GOOD "HORSE TRADE"

1855 Map of the Upper Peninsula of Michigan which Ohio traded for Toledo, showing several

WHEN PINE WAS KING

by

Lewis C. Reimann

Avery Color Studios
AuTrain, Michigan 49806

Dedication

This factual account of the early lumbering days in the Upper Peninsula of Michigan is affectionally dedicated to the lumberjacks, those hard, rugged men of the woods who bore the brunt of deep snow, freezing weather and the hardships in the crude lumber camps, often wet to the waist, and labored for mere subsistence to bring out the pine to build our early cities and homes. Many of these pioneers I knew, sometimes feared, yet greatly admired.

WHEN PINE WAS KING

by

Lewis C. Reimann

Copyright 1981
by
Avery Color Studios
AuTrain, Michigan 49806

First Edition - 1981
Reprinted - June 1983

Library of Congress No. 81-69704
ISBN 0-932212-24-7

All rights in this book are reserved. No part may be reproduced in any manner without permission in writing from the publisher, except brief quotations for review purposes.

WHEN PINE WAS KING was originally published in 1952 with copyright secured by Lewis C. Reimann.

Cover Photograph by Norton Louis Avery

Acknowledgments

Any author attempting to present the story of the early lumbering days in the Upper Peninsula of Michigan would be necessarily indebted to many old-timers and their descendants for tales and factual material, even though he may have witnessed some of the timber operations himself. Too many of these pioneers have passed from the scene to the loss of those who are interested in the beginnings in that dark land across the Straits of Mackinac.

Among those who have contributed the material in this book were John A. Lemmer, Victor A. Larsen, C. J. Sawyer and Kenneth Mallmann of Escanaba, Victor Lemmer of Ironwood, Rev. Lloyd Frank Merrell of Maurice, Jim Murphy of Elmwood, Allen Mercier, Charles Good and William Duchaine of Nahma, Deputy Sheriff Art Murray of Mio, George H. Hedquist of Detroit, James and John Bellaire of Manistique, John J. Riordan and Jack and Mrs. Sheriff William Schelm of Baraga, Carlos Reading of Ann Arbor, John Bellaire of Manistique, John J. Riordan and Jack and Mrs. Mitchell of Seney, Peter Madsen of Grayling, William Shingler of Kenton, Rev. James Roberts of South Lyon, Peter Peterson of Iron River, Otis Meehan of Buhl, Minnesota, and many others, some of whom are mentioned in the book.

The author is indebted for the pictures of the early lumber scenes to the Michigan Historical Collections and the School of Natural Resources of the University of Michigan, the Burton Historical Collections of Detroit and individuals.

To the above the author acknowledges his appreciation and thanks.

TABLE OF CONTENTS

Chapter 1	DARK LAND ACROSS THE STRAITS	13
Chapter 2	TREASURE STORE IN THE U.P.	18
Chapter 3	BILL BONIFAS—TIMBER KING	22
Chapter 4	THE TIMBER KING'S FORTUNE	32
Chapter 5	PINE AND POLITICS	41
Chapter 6	WHITE PINE SEPULCHERS	52
Chapter 7	WOODSMEN	60
Chapter 8	WHEN MEN WERE MEN	68
Chapter 9	FLEECING THE LUMBERJACK	83
Chapter 10	CHARACTERS OF THE NORTH	96
Chapter 11	THE VALLEY BOYS MEET THEIR MATCH	105
Chapter 12	BATTLE-SCARRED LUMBERJACKS	109
Chapter 13	WOMEN IN THE CAMPS	116
Chapter 14	BURIED TREASURE	122
Chapter 15	HORSEPOWER IN THE CAMPS	126
Chapter 16	THE PEGLEG MOOCHER	135
Chapter 17	SAM JACOBS-LUMBER CAMP JEWELER	137
Chapter 18	THE COUNTRY DOCTOR	144
Chapter 19	THE CROPPED EAR	154
Chapter 20	LOADED WITH DYNAMITE	156
Chapter 21	HONEY FOR THE BEAR	162
Chapter 22	THE PREACHER IN THE LUMBER CAMPS	166

The Pine Tree

by
Lloyd Frank Merrell

I might have seen the pine tree
Securely clasp the loam
To poise a harp of emerald
And crotch a squirrel-home.

I might have seen her jewels
At autumn's auction sale,
But I was blind computing
The lumber it would scale.

CHAPTER ONE

Dark Land Across the Straits

AN ARMY SERGEANT stabbed in the back with a penknife and two innocent farm horses were the only casualties in the "Bloodless Toledo War" but it resulted in giving Michigan a vast, dark, wild and fabulously rich empire called the Upper Peninsula, which in turn was the leader in various secession movements that may have brought about a new state in the Union or have lost that territory to Canada and the British Empire.

But little did the 23 year old boy governor of the Michigan Territory, Stevens T. Mason, know of the untold and undiscovered fortune that hung upon his actions when he ordered 1000 Michigan militiamen to Toledo to make arrests for any encroachments by the Ohio boundary commission and to fire on hostile military invaders in the summer of 1835.

The root of all the trouble was a map prepared in 1755 by Dr. John Mitchell which showed Lake Michigan to be forty miles too far north. This map was used for almost half a century and was even used by the United States and the British government in determining boundary questions following the Revolutionary War. Then the Northwest Ordnance of 1787 fixed the southern boundary of Michigan as an imaginary line drawn from the southern tip of Lake Michigan due east to the western tip of Lake Erie.

WHEN PINE WAS KING

When the borders of the new state of Ohio were defined in 1802, an old trapper and hunter from the Lake Michigan region pointed out to the Ohio delegation that the lake extended much farther south than the Mitchell map indicated. The Ohio politicians requested the federal officials to resurvey the area and prepare a map which would settle the matter forever. Their eyes were on the fast growing city of Toledo with its busy lake port in the mouth of the Maumee River. Congress directed surveyor William Harris to establish the new line in 1812. With the aid of a slightly curved line, Harris ended up with a new boundary which satisfied Ohio.

The Michigan Territory officials protested vigorously to President James Monroe, who ordered still another line surveyed by William A. Fulton, whose line ran due east from the tip of Lake Michigan and cut off Toledo and the Maumee River harbor giving them to Michigan. As a result both Ohio and Michigan claimed jurisdiction over the settlers in the disputed area and both tried to tax the confused citizens. Many refused to pay or even abide by the conflicting laws.

Border tension reached a peak in 1835. Ohio's Governor Robert Lucas requested his legislature to officially extend its jurisdiction to the Harris line. Governor Mason immediately took counter measures to prevent "organization of foreign jurisdiction within the limits of the territory of Michigan." Riots broke out in the area in defiance of the conflicting authorities. Ohio began mobilizing. Governor Mason called for volunteers to fight off the invasion. Mason sent General Joseph W. Brown with 1000 troops north of the Harris line. Lucas dispatched General Bell and 600 troops south of the Fulton line. The two governors, the two generals and the two armies maneuvered ferociously for weeks, each carefully refraining from crossing into the disputed territory and coming into armed conflict.

The first real engagement of the Toledo War took place at Phillips Field where 30 Michigan men captured four colonels, one major, one captain and three privates and took them as prisoners to Monroe. One night Michigan troops swooped down into the area and arrested Major B. F. Stickney, who drew a penknife and stabbed a slight wound in a Michigan sergeant's arm. Later two innocent farm horses strayed into the battle area at night and were shot.

Not to be outdone by this show of force, Governor Lucas sent a judge, a clerk and a small band of militiamen into the territory to hold court. They met in an abandoned schoolhouse. There by the light of a single candle no one spoke above a whisper. The meeting lasted only a few minutes but the Buckeyes hailed it as a moral victory. This evidence of authority was produced before President Andrew Jackson. Jackson decided to accept a compromise measure suggested by a Congressional Peace Commission. The Harris Line was set as the boundary between the warring states over the vigorous protest of Governor Mason and the Michigan legislature. However, politically strong Ohio, with representation in Congress as against the mere territorial status of Michigan, won the issue, but not until Michigan was given 9000 square miles of land belonging to the territory of Wisconsin, called thereafter the Upper Peninsula of Michigan, stretching east 261 miles from Wisconsin's border to Ontario and 104 miles from Lake Superior south to Lake Michigan.

WHEN PINE WAS KING

But Michigan people were not happy over this trade. It was a land "too far from civilization to ever amount to anything." One early settler in the U.P. called it God's Country.

"Yeah," yapped a critic. "It's God's country, all right. So few people live there that God alone looks after it."

To stop the wrangling and to hurry its petition for statehood which would give her political strength in Congress, Michigan settled for admission to the Union and other valuable considerations, including that wild, dark and unknown peninsula across the Straits of Mackinac. Wisconsin was the only loser and when she applied for admission into the Union, new agitation came from both sides of the UP-Wisconsin border for the inclusion of the UP in Wisconsin. It was a natural part of the latter's land body, they said. The center of the UP was closer to Madison, St. Paul and Chicago than to Lansing and Detroit. It's natural trade area was not Lower Michigan but Milwaukee, Green Bay and Chicago. The Straits of Mackinac formed a water barrier to close relations with the mother state. One Milwaukeean even suggested that the UP be taken into Wisconsin by force.

During the Civil War strong talk was again unloosened to following the South's lead in seceding from the Union. That threat was made on the floor of Congress. The reason: poor mail service. U.S. postal authorities came to the rescue with a new mail route. Furthermore, the Michigan legislature treated the UP like a stepchild. Few road improvements were made. Transportation was through mud and mire. Ferry service across the Straits was infrequent and undependable. Big-city legislators were the acknowledged enemies of any development in the UP. Even a Detroit newspaper admitted editorially:

"Perhaps the Upper Peninsula has not always been fairly treated."

Nothing came of the secession movement but the people of the UP had their last laugh. Their section was larger in area than Delaware, Connecticut and Massachusetts combined. It was soon producing one-third of the nation's iron ore; its pine land succeeded the depleted timber land production of the Lower Peninsula; in population, one of its cities—Calumet—became larger than any city in eight states of the Union. And there were more banks and deposits in the UP than in 18 states as the territory reached boom times.

It was only forty years later that the "horsetrade" with Ohio began to pay off. Since that time billions of dollars have been reaped from its vast forests of pine, hemlock and hardwoods, the deep copper mines on the shores of Lake Superior and the limitless beds of iron ore of the Marquette, Gogebic and Menominee Iron Ranges. Michigan gained in natural resources from that dark land across the Straits, fondly called "The Upper," far more than all the natural wealth of the whole state of Ohio.

What did Ohio gain on the trade?

Just Toledo!

CHAPTER TWO

Treasure Store in the UP

It was not until the early Seventies that men had begun to discover the untold riches which lay above and below the ground in the UP. Traders and trappers had indeed for over a hundred and fifty years gotten rich on the furs and the Indian trade there. John Jacob Astor of New York had established a chain of trading posts throughout the watercourses of the Great Lake, had switched his national allegiance from the colonies to the French, then to the colonies, then to the English again in order to safeguard his operations. The Hudson's Bay Company had posts in various spots in the UP from time to time. Copper had been dug from shallow mines of Isle Royale and had found its way to faraway Mexico before white men had begun to realize what wealth rested unexploited in the vast forests of pine and the iron and copper deposits deep in the ground.

It was a century and a half later that civilization pushed its way north to hack the giant pine which darkened the land across the straits from Wisconsin east to the St. Mary's River. As the pine of Maine became exhausted under the merciless demand for building timber and the seven pound axes of the lumberjacks, eyes turned to Michigan and its apparently inexhaustible resinous trees. The Saginaw Valley felt the first impact of the eastern timber speculators and loggers and lumberjacks who came from the east. Here they were joined by logging operators from Detroit and Chicago. Scores of lumber camps sent their billions of feet of logs down the Saginaw River and its great tributaries to the mills which lined the river banks.

The boom was on, not to be ended, they thought, as long as man lived. Fortunes poured into the coffers of dozens of operators. Saginaw, Bay City and neighboring towns became rip-roaring places almost overnight. Rough men from the camps and the mills filled the plank-walks to overflowing. Saloons lined the river banks and spread to the side streets. Houses of illfame followed the easy money and red-light districts flourished unrestricted. Give the men what they want—whiskey and women; keep the money in town, said the politicians and business men. If we don't get it someone else will. To hell with morals.

But the Saginaw boom was as shortlived as was the boom in the timberlands of Maine. The white pine was not inexhaustible. The timber dwindled with no thought of conservation or replanting. Let the idealists take care of that. Camps closed, towns died down, the lumberjacks and their employers moved north and west to find other "limitless" stands of the big stuff. West Branch, Grayling, Roscommon, Gaylord, Cadillac, Pellston and Mackinaw City boomed with the swelling tide. Timber kings, lumberjacks and camp followers rushed to these new areas, to cut, haul, exploit and steal the endless forests of the north. In their wake again came bust, ghost towns, wastelands, forest fires in the slashing, burned out soil and stranded families.

The hungry maw of the lumber mills was never satis-

A FORTUNE IN PINE

Camp operators bought forty acres of pine for from 65¢ to $1.25 an acre, or a total of $60.00, compared with today's price of $10,500.00

Burton Historical Collection

fied. Timber! Timber! Timber! was the cry. The cream was skimmed off the milk. Hardwoods were bypassed in the rush to supply pine lumber for the growing cities of Michigan, Illinois and the cities that lined the Great Lakes to Buffalo and beyond.

Soon men, equipment and supplies made their way by ferry boats and rail to the untapped pine land of the UP. The carnage left behind, the new dark land above the Straits of Mackinac was the next battle ground where the axe, the crosscut saw, the wide-bunked logging sleighs, giant Percheron and Belgian horses and huge ox teams were the materiel of the offensive. Escanaba, Germfask, St. Ignace, Trout Lake, Hermansville, Iron Mountain, Iron River, Watersmeet, Ironwood and other mushroom towns in the deep pine were the objectives of the attack.

French-Canadians from Quebec and New Brunswick, men from "Down Below," Swedes, Germans, Norwegians, and Finns from across the Atlantic, a powerful figure named Bill Bonifas from the little Duchy of Luxemburg and others, came to the new land to seek work and fortune—some to hack out millions in gold in the shape of pine, others to come away with just the clothes on their backs, others to be left in desolated towns after the battle had passed that way, to glean after the harvest the slim "pickin's" in the cutover and burned out areas of the north.

CHAPTER THREE

Bill Bonifas -- Timber King

IT MIGHT BE SAID of Bill Bonifas, the UP timber king, as Robert La Follette, the political nemesis of Philetus Sawyer, the Wisconsin lumber baron, senator and politician, said about the latter:—

"He believed in getting all he could for himself and his associates whenever and wherever possible. I always thought that Sawyer's methods did not violate his conscience; he regarded money as properly the chief influence in politics. Whenever it was necessary, I believe that he bought men as he bought saw-logs. He assumed that every man in politics was serving first of all his own personal interests—else why should he be in politics? He believed quite simply that railroads and lumber companies, as benefactors of the country, should be given unlimited grants of public lands, allowed to charge all the traffic could bear, and that anything that interfered with profits of business was akin to treason."

Despite the fortunes some lumber and timber kings made from their cheaply-bought private or public timber lands, wages continued to be pitifully low. Lumbermen joined in associations "to protect their interests." Demand for higher wages met with stubborn resistance and organized. The more intelligent "trouble makers" were placed on "blacklists" in all the cooperating camps. Wages in the woods continued to range from $16.00 to $30.00 a month plus food and a straw bunk to sleep in for labor six days a week from "portal to portal"—from the time the men left the camp in the dark of morning until they returned in the dark of night. Six days a week men saw no daylight in the camps. Sunday was a time for sharpening axes and tools, picking "crumbs" from their lice infested underwear and washing clothes.

Lumber camps attracted single men and families, businesses and professions to the lumber towns; investments in homes and business establishments were made; schools and township roads were built with taxpayers' money. Yet when the timber was denuded from the holdings, the operators moved to other, more attractive stands, leaving deserted homes, empty stores and abandoned families and the townships with heavy bonded indebtedness, with no means of retiring it.

Opportunities in the lumber region of the U.P. were limited to those timber enterprizers who were backed by wealth originating in Boston, New York or Chicago, as was often the case with the early companies in southern Michigan or Maine. Many individuals had had enough experience to start in on their own and anyone with the proper foresight and ambition could start with little in the woods and come out with much.

Nor were the opportunities limited to first-family Americans. Many immigrants from Europe found almost unlimited futures in the yet unexploited timber resources in that north country.

The little Duchy of Luxemburg, squeezed tightly between Germany, Belgium and France, like other European countries, furnished its quota of independent and ambitious citizens who sought their fortunes in the dark pine of the U.P.

One such person was William Bonifas who migrated to America as a tall, powerful young man, made his mark and left the impress and force of his character on the entire lumber industry of the mid-west and amassed a fortune which was said to have run from five to twenty million.

The son of a village blacksmith and six feet two in height and weighing in the neighborhood of 250 pounds, Bonifas landed from third class passage in New York dressed in an ill-fitting suit given him by a smaller Luxemburger, with sleeves which reached only half way to his wrists, a small bundle of clothes and a few American dollars in his pocket.

At the dock a labor agent told him of the need for workmen in the harvest fields of South Dakota and started him out on a freight train headed west. At Chicago Bonifas became confused by the many freight trains assembled there and took the wrong boxcar which landed him at Green Bay, Wisconsin. Finding no wheat fields there, he made inquiries in broken English about work opportunities in that north region. He was directed to Escanaba, a thriving mill town and iron ore shipping port in the late Eighties. At Escanaba he hired out to a railroad tie and fence post contractor to work in the swamps on the Garden Peninsula on the north shore of Lake Michigan, a few miles across the water from Escanaba.

Here he worked at "piece work" as a cutter of railroad ties and fence posts at a few cents apiece. A great rugged "greenhorn" who "never knew his own strength," ambitious to learn and earn quickly, he did the work of two men, cutting and carrying out from the swamps two heavy, sap-filled ties on his shoulders when other lesser men struggled to take out one. When the mile trip to the railroad siding or the boat dock proved too long, Bonifas bought a cheap horse and a mule to drag the stuff out. The horse proved weaker than the mule, so he made a shoulder harness for himself and helped the horse.

With long hours and abstemious habits he accumulated enough money to send for his three brothers and four sisters still living in the old family home in Luxemburg—John, James and Isaac and Lillian, Katherine, Mary and Celia. Together this sturdy family went into the lumber business in earnest. "Big Bill", as he was beginning to be called, set up a camp at Garden for 40 men. The sisters did the cooking, washing and the work entailed to keep the crew cared for and contented. The future Mrs. Bonifas, then an immigrant fresh from Ireland, served as a maid in the establishment.

Ties and fence posts came out of the swamps around Garden in millions and were boated across Big Bay de Noc to Escanaba for shipment by rail to Wisconsin and Illinois and by steamer to Detroit and other Great Lakes ports. Money rolled in faster than Bill could keep track of. He hired Mary Hogan, a teacher in the little town of Garden, as secretary of the company. A realistic and hard-bitten protector of the family finances, Bill trusted her completely and gave her authority over his affairs. She was the only person in the organization feared by the employees. She stayed with Bonifas all through his life and after his death became the beneficiary of a large part of his fortune, although, because of the investment opportunities her employer had given her, she left an estate of her own of $300,000.00 or more.

When the timber at Garden had been stripped and Bonifas had accumulated a considerable reserve, estimated by some at around $125,000.00, he sought timber land farther north in the U.P. At Watersmeet, and Marenesco he bought great tracts of virgin pine, cedar, hemlock, balsam and spruce. He opened an operation at a location called Bonifas. He employed several hundred men in his various camps and was known as "The Timber King" in all the lumber industry.

Pine land was cheap and could be bought for from sixty-five cents to a dollar and a half an acre. The booming cities and towns of the middle west as well as the east were demanding more and more white and Norway pine, while the railroads were extending and buying ties by the millions. The paper industry was new but chewed up pulpwood as fast as it could be produced.

The Kimberly-Clark Paper Company, operating several mills in Wisconsin, turned to Bonifas for raw material and joined with him to establish the United Lumber Company, paying him an alleged price of $250,000.00 in paper mill stock for his holdings. Bonifas at no time operated a saw mill. His field was cutting, hauling and shipping logs, ties and fence posts to his outlets. He was no "lumber king." He was a "Timber King" alone. He continued as manager of the new lumber company at a handsome salary. His stock in the paper company was his major source of income, for during the first World War Kimberly-Clark had a virtual monopoly of the pulpwood market and were able to set their own price for paper and pulp.

WHEN PINE WAS KING

As his fortune piled beyond his wildest expectations, Big Bill sought investments. He bought stock in the Scripps-Booth Car Company which was having a hard time in competition with the big automobile manufacturers.

When the company was near bankruptcy, General Motors Corporation bought its plant and machinery, giving Bonifas stock in payment for his shares. This added greatly to his holdings and eventually was his greatest source of income. Kimberly-Clark and Bonifas joined in the purchase of 180 acres of land in Texas and found oil there later. Together they owned a bank in Seattle which was said to have netted the lumberman more money than his timber operations. His timber interests spread to Winnegar, Wisconsin and to Lake Linden in the Copper Country.

Thus the big, rugged immigrant from Luxemburg piled fortune on fortune from his ventures in pine, ties, fence posts, oil and paper. No single person knew the extent of his holdings or the amount of accumulations but Mary Hogan, his faithful watchdog of the treasury, who died after Bonifas' death but before the timber king's will was probated. Mary never revealed her knowledge but the fortune was estimated from five to twenty millions.

Having "come up the hard way," Big Bill was never suspected of being a spendthrift. When Victor Lemmer, a former favorite employee, was married, Bonifas and his wife attended the party. After the ceremony the children of the neighborhood gathered at the home to bell the couple and to obtain treats. Members of the wedding party threw money to the kids. Bonifas pulled a half dollar from his pocket to throw in, looked at it, then placed it back in his pocket. As the money continued to flow out, he again reached for the silver piece and threw it in, saying:—

"Oh, hell."

A millionaire, many times over! Oh, hell!

Whenever he traveled about on business his wife packed his lunch to eat on the way. A millionaire!

Big Bill loved sports and attended a boxing match in Escanaba accompanied by his brother John. When one of the boxers failed to appear, the manager asked for volunteers to come into the ring to take on a toughy from Milwaukee. John urged Bill to try. Stripped to the waist and showing his bulging chest, he climbed into the ring. He swung a haymaker in the second round and knocked out his opponent. And that without using calked boots, as he had often done on subduing a burly lumberjack in his camps.

It was only during his last years that Bonifas used much of his wealth for his own enjoyment and the pleasure of his friends. He learned late how to play golf, but he was more skilled in the use of a canthook than a putter, and his lumber dealer friends soon learned that he was more glib at lumberjack language than golf terms.

He was asked repeatedly:

"Why do you keep on working so hard? You don't need more money. Why don't you play a little now?"

His usual reply was:—

"I just enjoy making money."

Big Bill's only extravagance was the erection of a fabulous lodge on the shore of Lake Gogebic, close to the scene of his big timber operations. Here the county built a wide road leading to the resort. The road was later closed and became a private thoroughfare despite the fact that it was built at county expense. It was at this lodge that he elaborately entertained business tycoons and government officials. Local, county, state and federal office holders were good friends to have when questions of taxation, elections, court suits and property lines were in questions.

The big lodge was the scene of the visit by Edna Ferber when the author was gathering material for her novel, "Come and Get It," a rip-roaring volume of the early lumbering days that presented the exploits and methods of the lumber barons in none too favorable a light. Even the lodge was turned into cash later when it was sold to become "The 500 Bushel Club," now operated as the "Northern Holiday," owned by Funk and Sons Seed Company of Kentland, Indiana.

In his latter days Bonifas traveled with a chauffeur. When he stayed at a hotel he had a cot placed in his room for the chauffeur to sleep on. It cost less than two rooms! When they entered the hotel he directed the chauffeur to buy a newspaper from the elevator boy, for it cost one cent less than at the news counter.

On one occasion he made the trip to Chicago in company of a friend from Escanaba. He drove the car to the entrance of the hotel and requested his friend to wait until his return, then disappeared through the hotel entrance. The friend waited all day and into the night in the car before parking the car and securing a room in the hotel. The friend drove the car to the hotel entrance the next morning, waited all day again, with no signs of Bonifas. The next morning as he drove the car around again, Bonifas appeared, got into the car and drove back to Escanaba, with no word of explanation asked or given.

Bonifas has no children, though one of his brothers had ten sons. The family worked together through the early days but did not fare as well as they expected at the probate of the timber king's will. Bonifas gradually withdrew from lumber operations, gave his time to guarding his fortune, warding off applicants of gifts for various causes and charities. He retired in 1932 and died in 1936 at the age of 67, leaving his entire wealth to his wife.

Mrs. Bonifas was entirely a homebody. Born in Ireland in 1864, she came of modest beginnings and was retiring and reserved all her life, in direct contrast to her self-confident, extrovert husband. Beginning as a maid with the Bonifas family, she continued her self-effacement despite the position her husband's wealth might have given her. From the day of her marriage she did all of her own housework, the scrubbing, baking and shopping. She maintained few social contacts and those only with women of like background. She regularly baked twice a week, cooked for her husband, housecleaned and darned her own stockings. She did not employ a maid until she was 83 years of age. She had no conception of the amount of her wealth. She had always dealt in small numbers. Large figures confused her.

Bonifas had acquired a swank home in Miami Beach which they occupied winters in their latter years. A caller had occasion to see Mrs. Bonifas there. As he approached the home he saw a woman scrubbing the steps in front of the house.

"I called to see Mrs. Bonifas," he said.

WHEN PINE WAS KING

"I am Mrs. Bonifas," the woman replied, wringing the suds from her red hands and led the visitor into the palatial home.

CHAPTER FOUR

The Timber King's Fortune

THE FORTUNE left by Big Bill Bonifas, the timber king, was a source of confusion and embarrassment to his widow. Accustomed to dealing with small amounts of money, she had left all money matters to her late husband.

The price of strawberries at the little grocery store on the corner in Escanaba brought her to wrath. On one occasion she asked the clerk:—

"What price berries today?"

"Strawberries are scarce this year. These are 49 cents today."

Turning on her heel, she stalked out of the store.

On the death of her husband, Mrs. Bonifas faced a dilemna. Friends, beggars, churches, colleges and others sought her out for sizeable gifts. She resented people asking her direct for money. A Mother Superior from Milwaukee came to her and demanded that she give $100,000.00 to build an orphanage. Mrs. Bonifas became so incensed at this direct demand that she asked the Mother to leave her house. However, should anyone come to tell her about some good cause or project without asking for assistance, she always had the matter carefully investigated. Should the cause be worthy she gave generously.

As demands and requests kept piling up to her utmost confusion, Mrs. Bonifas turned to John A. Lemmer, a former employee of Bonifas and the superintendent of schools of Escanaba for 32 years. He was asked to become her personal secretary and financial advisor. A man of broad educational and social interests, he became her sole confidant in the dispensing of her husband's wealth. She relied upon him completely. To protect himself, Lemmer suggested that he furnish her with his personal bond and to have an audit made of her finances before he began his duties. She turned the suggestion aside:—

"If I didn't trust you, I wouldn't have you as my secretary."

However, she acceded to his request.

Again Mrs. Bonifas revealed her lack of large figures. Lemmer held a few shares of Kimberly-Clark stock. Bonifas had acquired many. Lemmer owned a few. One dividend check for $23,000.00 from Kimberly-Clark came to Mrs. Bonifas. She asked Lemmer how much he had received from the same source.

"$13.00," he replied.

"That's nice," she said innocently.

Mrs. Bonifas' car had a puncture. That evening she called Lemmer to her home, complained bitterly that she had been charged $1.50 for the repair. Before the evening was over she directed him to write out checks of $30,000.00 for charities.

The influence of the superintendent of schools and confidential secretary was evident in the gifts Mrs. Bonifas made during her lifetime and the generous provisions of her will. No city in the United States of the size of Escanaba has ever been the beneficiary of so large gifts from any estate or individual.

During his lifetime Bonifas had made a number of

sizeable gifts to St. Joseph's Catholic Church and gymnasium in Escanaba and a large gift toward the completion of the engineering building at Marquette University of Milwaukee. However, the great bulk of the fortune was left for the widow to distribute personally and through her will under the wise advise and counsel of John Lemmer.

After the death of her husband, Mrs. Bonifas gave the Katherine Bonifas Technical School to the Escanaba Board of Education and swore the Board to secrecy as to the source. This made for a difficult problem. The Board was spending thousands of dollars building the school while the teachers in the school system were underpaid.

"Here," the teachers complained, "the board is spending the taxpayers' money without a vote, yet teachers receive no raise."

Public pressure became so great that Mrs. Bonifas was requested to allow the matter be made public.

Her charities and gifts during her latter years were many. She requested Lemmer to visit the little village of Garden, where she and her husband had made their start in life and where she had served as a maid, to learn what was most needed there. He made an investigation and reported to her that a new school was the greatest need. She was a loyal and devoted Catholic and ninety per cent of the children at Garden were Catholic. She thought immediately of building a parochial school. Lemmer pointed out that the Protestant children would thereby be left to attend the delapidated little public school. She proceeded to have a public school built.

She also built a chapel at Holy Cross Cemetery in Escanaba. Upon her death in 1948 she was the first person interred there. Her will revealed a total of over $2,500,000.00 in gifts to her many charities, members of her family, the city and schools, friends and Catholic churches and projects. All recipients were paid one hundred per cent of the will provisions, with the residue going to the Roman Catholic Bishop of the Diocese of Marquette, the Board of Education of Escanaba and the city of Escanaba to share equally.

The will gave the Bonifas residence as headquarters for priests engaged in missionary work in the U.P.; $11,000.00 to priests in several parishes in the U.P.; a life annuity of $150.00 per month to a niece; $68,000.00 in personal bequests to relatives and friends; the household and personal property to the executor; $253,000.00 to Catholic causes, colleges and other; $600,000.00 for the building of a Catholic high school; $100,000.00 for a home for Catholic old people; $150,000.00 for an elementary public school at Garden; $500,000.00 for a public senior high school; $20,000.00 to maintain the Katherine Bonifas Technical School; $150,000.00 to build a school for handicapped children; $100,000.00 toward a Junior College; $50,000.00 in scholarships for worthy high school graduates; $100,000.00 toward a combined city hall and county courthouse; and $100,000.00 to recreational facilities for the city of Escanaba.

Thus ended the life and fortune of one of the most fabulous timber kings in America. Other even greater fortunes were hacked out of Michigan's rich pine resources to be distributed to descendants but little enjoyed as riches by the men who found joy and satisfaction only in the struggle. But few were as liberal or as wise in the final distribution of their wealth as was the big man who had

THE PIECE-CUTTERS' CAMP

These men cut railroad ties and fence posts "by the piece." One-man saws, axes and a peeling spud were the chief tools used.

U. of Mich. School of Natural Resources

WINTER WOODS WERE BEAUTIFUL
But the work was rugged, the life monotonous, the food coarse, the hours long, the pay low.
Burton Historical Collection

CUTTING THE LOGS

These men worked with axes, saws, steel wedges, sledges and measuring sticks, knee deep in snow.
Burton Historical Collection

CUTTING "ROUND FORTIES"
Some operators bought one forty of pine and cut all the surrounding forties by trespass.
Burton Historical Collection

migrated from a humble blacksmith's home in the Duchy of Luxemburg. Most of Michigan fortunes from pine have gone into other family investments, some to lead soft living and eventual failure on the part of those who need not struggle to wrest a living the hard way.

CHAPTER FIVE

Pine and Politics

Numberless are the tales of big pine steals in the early days of the UP. That dark land across the Straits had 20,664 square miles of land surface, all but eighteen percent covered by pine and hardwoods. In some sections the pine stood 50-60-70- and 80-feet to the first limb. The average yield per acre was six thousand board or four million feet per square mile. Here was timber enough, they said, to supply the building needs of the whole country for generations to come. Yet within fifteen short years the UP's inexhaustible pine was merely a memory. There were small stands here and there owned by private individuals as a reminder of what once was.

The U.S. Land Office was profligate in its gifts of miles of pine land to railroad and canal companies. To encourage the development of the country these corporations were granted every odd section along their right of way or were given every odd section in parts of the UP for promised construction of railroads and canals, some of which were begun but never completed. Of its fifty-five million acres the UP lost over one fourth of its timber land in that way.

Timber operators at times bought a forty or section of pine land, set up their camps, sent crews into the woods to fell the trees, haul the logs to the rollways on the river bank or to the railroad siding. Ownership lines meant next to nothing unless the land office inspectors or individual owners of adjacent land kept close watch over the cuttings.

When cutters came to the property line and asked where the limits were the foreman often replied:—

"When you come up to the blaze, look as far as you can, then cut up to there."

"Round Forties" were the rule in many instances. "Cut your own forty and all the forties around it."

A small operator, Paul Minckler in the Iron River district, bought a forty of timber land from the land office and continued to cut another government forty. This was reported to the land office. Minckler learned of the impending investigation and knew that if he were convicted he would be subject to a fine of three times the value of the stolen timber. He induced a woman of questionable character to file a claim on the trespassed land and live there the required six months to "prove up" on her holding. He paid her $1.25 per acre at the end of the period and she in turn paid the land office, taking out a deed in her own name. When she had secured title she filed suit against Minckler for trespass and cutting the timber on her claim. She collected three times the value of the timber and land.

One of the timber kings of Michigan whose name is on many buildings and monuments in one of the old lumbering cities of the state bought school land and made small down payments, then cut off all the timber, abandoned the land without paying the balance, thus building up a fabulous fortune.

He hired dummy homesteaders to file on a quarter section of pine land and clear a small woods lot as a gesture toward improving the claim. The alleged homesteader allowed the timber baron to cut all the pine. When it came time to prove up on the property and acquire title, he would disappear. Upon investigation by the land office it was found that the timber had been cut and hauled out and the dummy had moved to parts unknown. The operator could show that he had bought the timber in good faith by producing a bill of sale. Only stumps and burned over land were left, thus the schools of the whole state were robbed of millions of dollars before too-late laws and stringent supervision were established.

In some counties taxes were levied by the board of supervisors on company owned land with the consent of the lumber companies to induce the building of roads in the vicinity of their operations. The roads once built, the taxes were never paid, throwing the burden of the road bonds back on the settlers in the counties.

More than one U.S. ex-land agent and many associated speculators were reported to have acquired great wealth in extensive and valuable tracts of pine by means of bogus pre-emption and fraudulent means. Since homestead laws gave every bona fide settler an opportunity of acquiring 160 acres of land as a free gift the pre-emption law scarcely served any other purpose than a cover to fraud. Large and choice tracts of pine were fraudulently entered under the pre-emption law by persons in the employ of companies and speculators in order to give them a semblance of compliance with the regulations and requirements as to settlement. One large corporation of land speculators provided portable houses which were easily moved about from one desirable quarter to another until the timber was cut off. Systematically much of our pine land was "mined off" in this way.

On June 1, 1881 the state of Michigan granted to the Detroit, Mackinac & Marquette RR 1,400,000 acres of land in payment of a railroad from the Straits of Mackinac to Marquette upon the completion of the said road. At the same time the D.M. & M. RR floated a loan of $18,000,000.00 for the building of the railroad. Thus the railroad acquired land, timber and mineral rights for the sum of about $1.25 per acre, which in turn it sold for many times that amount to loggers and farmers along the right of way.

The railroad from Marquette to L'Anse is 63 miles in length. The railroad company was granted every odd numbered section along its right of way for building the road, which thereby entitled it to 327,000 acres but it actually took possession of 540,000 acres, an extra 213,-000 of valuable timber and mineral land.

The stripped land was allowed to revert to the state for non-payment of taxes when nothing valuable was left to exploit. In 1897 C. V. DeLand, the Michigan Tax Statistician, recommended to the legislature that no less than six counties containing 200 townships should be consolidated with other counties for the reason that with the removal of their pine resources their taxable property, i.e., their pine timber, together with its present owners, had so far disappeared that there was not enough taxable property that could be realized by the assessors to maintain the expense of operating their county governments.

Timber kings were interested in one thing and one thing only. Caring nothing about the country and its future but to cut and slash their way ruthlessly through the standing pine and make a quick fortune. A veteran logger characterized the transition of land from public to private ownership as "one of the greatest periods of graft and exploitation that this nation has ever gone through. The rule was to beat the other fellow before he beat you and it was followed with a conscientiousness born of greed and avarice." Their slogan was "Wealth is for those who know how to get it."

In one of the large townships in western UP a small timber contractor controlled local politics as the stooge of the big timber king operating in the area. He kept a tight curb over the school district. His wife was regularly elected as secretary of the school board while he was always a member of the board of supervisors. No superintendent of schools stayed longer than two years if he refused to cooperate with the politicians. The political boss purchased supplies for the school and gave generous amounts of them to his friends. Should the superintendent object to this procedure his contract was promptly cancelled.

The board of supervisors assessed the land and business properties of the big lumber company and the politicians rode around in big automobiles. Little attention was paid to election laws. When the election of the stooges was in jeopardy the timber king brought 400 or 500 lumberjacks into town to vote in the township election. No business or professional man whose income was dependent upon the lumber industry dared to oppose the machine. No voter was ever challenged except those known to be opposed to the graft and these were dealt with harshly.

An Armenian railroad employee spent most of his time

in political maneuvering and little time at his job. He stood in well with the timber king and the railroad which overlooked sharp practices in exchange for fat log and lumber shipping contracts. He knew the power of the big political boss and asked to be appointed head of the township poor commission and its lucrative deals. Eighty others wanted the appointment. The board of supervisors decided that all names would be placed in a hat and the lucky person would receive the position. As chairman of the board the boss palmed the slip containing the Armenian's name and drew it out of the hat.

Strict control of local politicians who assessed the value of the timber lands and camp properties was essential to the timber kings. When that was the case assessments ranged from five to fifteen percent of their actual value. After the land was denuded of merchantable timber and fires ravaged the cut-over land, the timber kings allowed the land to revert back to the state for unpaid taxes, or sold the land to gullible farmers for from $1.00 to $2.50 an acre, thus realizing their original investment.

Thick standing pine land could be bought from the state land office for from sixty-five cents to $1.50 an acre. The average forty acres yielded around 300,000 board feet of lumber, thus for $60.00 a timber buyer could purchase pine which in 1952 would cost him $10,500.00 when bought "on the stump" from the Federal Forest Preserves.

At times Indian-owned land was bought for its timber for a paltry sum and the ownership allowed to remain in possession of the Indians in order that no taxes could be levied on the purchaser. Indian agents in some instances became wealthy by their conniving.

Lumber companies were not above stealing logs and timber from each other. As logs were piled on the river banks in rollways, scalers for the operators would measure the board feet in each log with their Scribner Rule, set down the figures in their books and mark the end of the log with a hammer bearing the logger's insignia. Should the scaler do his measuring in the late afternoon, the foreman would promise to roll the logs into the river the next morning. The camp crew then worked at night and dumped the logs into the river to a boom. A crew down river pulled the logs out of the river, cut off the ends and rolled them up in a pile on the river bank. The next morning the scaler, thinking it was another cut, would scale the same logs and give credit to the logger. The scaler's figures were always accepted as accurate by the buyer who was none the wiser.

When the lumber companies trespassed onto adjoining timber, suits were instituted by the owners. While the matter rested in the courts the cutting continued, with the operators telling the owners:—

"By the time the court decides the trees will be cut and all you'll have left is the stumps. You better settle at our price."

When government owned timber land was put up at auction, dozens of operators and speculators flocked to the land office to outbid each other. This sent the price up to such an extent that it was no longer as profitable to secure timber. The buyers then formed a ring whereby only one would make a bid on each piece, thus enabling them to buy at ridiculously low prices. Each member of the ring, too, had his turn at bidding so each would get a good buy.

WHEN PINE WAS KING

Registers of local land offices were often corrupt and the General Land Office rather lax. Most people of the time condoned the practice of the rings. They seemed forgiving enough in face of the outright theft of timber from the state, federal and private land. It brought business into the area. "You can't outsmart money."

The township of Watersmeet in the western end of the UP was the scene of political conniving, scheming and bribery. A big lumber company operated there. When it appeared that politics and assessment rates could no longer be easily controlled, the southern half of the township was split off and made into Nelson township. Here the lumber king had complete control of elections. Lumberjacks, some with no homes of their own, drifters from camp to camp, were registered and released from work on election day to vote company officers and their stooges into township offices. Assessments were reduced to a few cents on the dollar. Lumbering went on apace until the timber was skimmed off in the most wasteful manner, the cedar, hemlock and pulpwood cut and shipped to the mills below. Slashings of denuded land were left behind to burn in the frequent forest fires which raged each dry summer.

After the cheaply bought timber had been harvested and the land had become valueless, the barren township of Nelson was turned back once more to become a part of Watersmeet township. The abandoned families now faced the double dilemma of little or no work and additional taxes for the upkeep of roads and schools and such public services as were needed. The timber king retired to hoard his investments in banks, railroads, paper mills and General Motors stock. Little or nothing of value remained in the impoverished township, while the exploiter left his millions to charities and his church after his death.

Not all timber fortunes were made by cutting and milling pine. Timber men who were early on the scene, seeing the future demands for lumber in the rapidly growing midwest, bought up great tracts of timber land for speculation for a few dollars an acre, held it a few years, then sold it at greatly increased prices.

Philetus Sawyer, timber king and Wisconsin politician, who operated in Wisconsin and the UP, with a fortune of a quarter of a million in 1869, doubled his wealth every five years. He bought one tract for $1500.000 and sold it within a few years for $63,000.00. He bought another for $7000.00 and sold it for $84,000.00. Another cost him $16,000.00 and sold for $120,000.00.

Political maneuvering by lumber kings did not stop with the end of the pine era. One such family moved to Detroit where their investments set up new and greater fortunes to be lavished on their children to their ruination. The second generation head of the family attempted to buy his way into the U.S. Senate by spending over a million and a half dollars to secure his election, only to have the Senate deny him a seat. Sawyer, however, was more astute and rose from Wisconsin legislator to the U.S. Senate and complete control of the Republican party.

Lumber men like Sawyer and U.S. Senator Ike Stephenson of Wisconsin were instrumental in passing land laws which made the rape of timber lands complete.

One timber king, known as Big Jack, was married but had no legitimate progeny. A rugged, handsome man, away from home most of the year, he was attractive to other women with the result that it was easy for him to stray from the narrow path of virtue. The wife of his bookkeeper was one of his amours. Her son was the spitting image of Big Jack. Her husband, working for a modest salary, lived lavishly. How many off-spring Big Jack had was anyone's guess and there was much guessing as new babies were born in the area. He operated several lumber camps and his wanderings were wide.

One evening the bookkeeper was crying into his beer in a saloon. Becoming maudlin over his liquor and his troubles with his wife, he showed a friend a check for $7000.00 which he said was hush money from the lumberman to keep his big mouth shut.

"That such and such," he cried. "He thinks he can keep me quiet with a measley $7000.00. There's lots more where this came from and I'll get it."

The limitless forests of pine stretching from Ironwood to Marquette and east beyond "would never be exhausted", they said in the late Eighties. The cutting, driving and milling continued through the Nineties until the UP's white pine gave out, the lumber camps closed and ghost towns remained behind with its people stranded, the fortunes moved to the big cities to be reinvested in banks, railroad stock and the young automobile industry.

Where once tall pine had stood dark and vast there now stretched vast tracts of wasteland. The cut-over areas were littered with refuse from the hasty, grabbing lumbering; fire burned off what was left of brush and stumps; the unprotected topsoil was washed away by erosion; a wild tangle of pin cherries and hazel brush grew up in the scorched ground to be again exposed to frequent and destructive attacks by fire. The area offered no fit habitation for man or beast. Here and there a former lumberjack or trusting immigrant bought a piece of high ground from the deserting lumber operators to eke out a precarious living from the bare soil, the few stands of cedar in the swamps and the game which had escaped the whirlwind of lumbering and fire.

Having harvested the money from the trees, many of the lumbermen, young and energetic enough, moved on to the new stands of virgin timber in the Pacific Northwest to begin all over again their destructive and wasteful exploitation of a natural resource still unprotected by government control. They left behind them their rubbish for the conservationists to worry about. The lumbermen who remained behind to enjoy their riches in the cities were no more concerned than those who had abandoned the scene for new fields and woods to conquer.

CHAPTER SIX

White Pine Sepulchers

As the ravishing and destruction of the UP's pine was in progress, there were a few individuals who stood by helplessly watching, idealists and socially-conscious people, unable to stem the tide of waste of a people's natural resources. Timber kings were powerful. State and federal officials connived in the devastation and squandering of the rich heritage given up so readily by the productive land.

One man of literary talent witnessed the carnage and lent his ability through poetry to point out the scene when it was too late.

Reverend Lloyd Frank Merrell, a preacher in that vast country, was like a voice crying in the destroyed wilderness. After most of the butchery of our pine was practically completed he put the scene into verse:—

Cut-over sepulchers, your spirit is
A widow hunched with grief who rosaries
Each calvaried son with brooding agonies.

Your breasts once velvety full are cracked and spent.
You seem to yearn for days of old content
When sturdy tongues absorbed their nourishment.

WHEN PINE WAS KING

My aching pity joins the fitful tide
Of anguish menacing on every side
From one whose heart is flaming open wide.

Woodfolk are trapped in clearing and swamp with blaze
Of sudden wrath that leaves a threatening haze
Of terror over jackpine plains for days.

I check your fiery spasms. You have a name
For being moody. Watchmen eye your frame
In haunting dread of any lurking flame.

I will not look askance and call you hag,
Although your mourning weeds, charred rag on rag,
Shroud amputated stump and crippled snag.

The molten slit that hardly could contain
Your pangs is cooled by equinoctial rain.
The heavens are kind to you who seem in pain.

Often your eyes go wild and sleety brine,
Stinging like fire on whirlwind tempests, whine
Through bald scrub oak for massacre of pine.

Green leaves evaded storms but not the race
Of zero greed. Heart-sick, I hold my place
And take my bitter scourge upon your face.

Timber! You groaned and trembled over the yell
Of gloating lumberjacks when martyrs fell
And years of grandeur fed the fires of hell.

THE HAULING SLEIGH

These sleighs had runners 4 inches wide and 7 inches deep; beams between runners were 10" x 14"; the bunks holding the logs were from 8' to 12' wide to hold enormous loads.

Burton Historical Collection

THE CROSS HAUL

A team pulled the logs up skids by means of a decking chain. Quick skill with a cant hook was required by the top-loaders.

Burton Historical Collection

READY TO ICE THE ROAD

When roads were iced, a gouger was used to cut ruts in the ice the width of the sleigh runner to prevent the sleigh from leaving the road.

Burton Historical Collection

LOADING THE SPRINKLER
Iced logging roads were essential for hauling great loads to the rollways. A team drew the barrel from water hole to fill the tank.
Burton Historical Collection.

WHITE PINE SEPULCHERS

From winter's prison house of firm control
Your tears, unlocked by spring, whirlpool and roll
Through drifted grief to ease a pent-up soul.

You place a trillium wreath around the thrones
Of fallen kings, arbutus on the stones,
And rouge with raspberries your pale cheek bones.

Cloud-ladies robed in white observe with mirth
The strawberries my widow brings to birth
To tint her pallid, sandy lips of earth.

In carmine smile the berry I behold
With reverence the Cosmic Will unfold
A dream of ravished woodlands turned to gold.

I glimpse your patient soul in leafy eyes
Of quivering aspen prayers of yours that rise
For infant pines to brave unfriendly skies.

New boughs appear. You have become your god.
Discard the ebony weeds. Blueberry sod
Is cradling sons where patriarchs have trod.

Leaves breathing ozone, roots in humus clay,
The pines with starry goal exult and sway
Their banners over wrecks of yesterday.

The porcupine, the partridge, fox and deer
That fled the ax and gun of the pioneer
Seem glad for homes of pine to reappear.

WHEN PINE WAS KING

Your spring-fed brooks of even temperature
Reveal a love inviolate and pure.
The love I give to you will not endure.

But other hearts will vow you are their own.
Blue crags were never made to brood alone.
Such rugged wilds could melt a heart of stone.

Unloose your charm. The widow years are done.
Upon the loom of dreams your leaves have spun
An emerald trousseau, new bride of the sun.

CHAPTER SEVEN

Woodsmen

As the timber operations in the UP developed, woodsmen came in from all directions—from the woods of New Brunswick and Quebec came French-Canadians, from the cutover land of the Saginaw Valley, Grayling and Cadillac, from across the Atlantic—England, Germany, Sweden, Finland, Norway and the Baltic countries. Here was a new, virgin area awaiting rugged men and timber kings to cut and mill the giant white and cork pine that stood dark across the Straits of Mackinaw.

French-Canadians came first with the heavy axes, colorful head gear and bright scarves. They were unacquainted with the use of a saw to fell trees. The Finns, who followed closely on their heels, introduced the saw as a means of rapidly toppling over trees and cutting them into proper sawlog lengths. These blond giants from the north region of Europe were large, rugged men, accustomed to long hours of work in snow and freezing weather and were more docile than the quick-tempered men from Canada.

The men from "Down Below," southern Michigan, came up to the new country with a swagger, for had they not made a clean sweep of the pine there, drank the most whiskey and loved the most women? Brawls, fights and good natured rivalry sprang up between these men from the scattered areas. The French-Canadian was dubbed a "frog"; the men from across the pond were "greenhorns" and "hunkies", the Saginaw toughs were "The Valley Boys". A few city men tried their hand at woods work and had a hard time of it under the jibes of the hardened timber workers. Men new to the ways of the camps came in for much practical joking. They were sent for left-handed monkey wrenches, round squares, shore lines, and ricochets. When they asked a jack for the articles they were told that one of the others had just used it. They went from one person to another until it dawned upon them that they were having their leg pulled.

The first time a greenhorn went to the tarpaper-covered privy back of the men's camp, he yelled for toilet paper. One of the old jacks yelled back:

"Listen to the dude!"

Joe Courtney was the ward of Tom Nestor, a lumberman in the Houghton country. Joe attended Notre Dame University. Upon graduation he came to work for Nestor in one of his camps.

One Saturday evening when he was in town he received an invitation from Jerry Real, the local druggist, to attend a square dance at the home of Cadotte, an Indian fiddler. Being unfamiliar with the local lumber town customs, Joe asked Real what he should wear.

"Why, this is always a real fancy affair at Cadotte's on Saturday night, so dress formal!"

Joe put on his tuxedo and stiff-front shirt and a black bow tie. Upon entering Cadotte's home he found all the men dressed in stag pants, work shirts and lumbercamp shoes. He became the butt of jokes and rough jibes immediately. The big lumberjacks bumped into him on the dance floor, stepped on his dance pumps and pulled off his black bow tie. The boys were hitting the bottle enthusiastically and the party became rough. Joe received a thorough roughing and didn't know where to turn for support. This was a new kind of party. Notre Dame with its wild students had never given him such a time.

In the middle of a square dance one of the jacks spit a quid of tobacco onto Joe's stiff shirt front. Someone dropped a bottle of whiskey onto the dance floor where it broke. Cadotte incensed at such waste started a fight. One of the Indians came in with a long barreled rifle to stop the fight.

Joe looked around desperately and yelled:—

"This is no place for a college boy! I'm getting out!"

A window was open. He dove through head-first and ran back to Tom Nestor's home.

Dickie Coogan, "The Gardener", got his nickname from his method of getting pay for the work he never did. An old, retired lumberjack, he spent his time in the saloons begging drinks from the bartenders and the flush lumberjacks until his goodwill ran out. He was a harmless little man, ordinarily, but a man had to eat and drink.

A town woman hired Dickie to spade and plant her garden. Each day he asked her for money to buy seed, then proceeded to drink it up in the taverns. As the time for the seed to come up approached, the woman watched her garden plot daily but no plants appeared. By the middle of the summer the ground bore only a nice stand of rank weeds. One morning she decided to run Dickie down for an explanation. She knew where to find him—

sitting on a high bank with the other idle lumberjacks waiting for smoke to appear out of the saloon chimneys, indicating that the bartender had arrived.

Facing Dickie the woman demanded what happened to the seeds she had paid for.

"B' damn," replied Dickie sheepishly, "I was so thirsty I spend the money in the saloon. I jus' forgot to get the seed."

Bill Gingway, a big, powerful Indian, lived in a shack in the woods. He worked as a lumberjack and river hog for the Bay de Noc Lumber Company whose headquarters were at Nahma on the north shore of Lake Michigan. He had made his stake in one of Fred Good's camps and came down by log train to Nahma to cash his time slip and buy supplies for the summer. He treated some of his camp buddies at the only saloon the Bay de Noc Company allowed in the company-owned town. Before he started back home he had a double load—food and "interior decorations."

Bill headed for the log train with a jug in his hand when Fred met him.

"Bill," said Fred, "you've got load enough on your back and inside you. I can't allow you to take that jug of whiskey on the train to camp."

Bill meekly turned back to the company grocery store and presently returned to the train carrying a kerosene can.

Fred was wise to what Bill was carrying in the can but remarked to the conductor standing by:

"Let him on, if he's that smart."

Ed Guertin, a French-Canadian, ran a camp 30 miles from Nahma but was having trouble getting men to work in the woods. The camp was too far from liquor supplies. He came to Allen Mercier, foreman for the Bay de Noc Company, for advice.

"I got plentee timber-r-r. I got plentee team. I got plentee chuck in camp, but I can't get them god damn logs out wit'out men. Can't you get me some jacks, Allen?"

Mercier, anxious to have the timber cut and shipped to his company's mill at Nahma, contacted a Milwaukee employment office and asked them to ship up some of their unemployed city men.

Twenty-four men came up on the train dressed in city clothes—low oxfords, thin socks, cotton shirts, thin gloves—apparel unfit for snow, wet weather and freezing temperatures. Unaccustomed to the northern Michigan climate, the men produced little timber but bitter complaints for having been brought to the woods by golden promises of good wages and ideal work conditions.

Guertin again took the log train back to Nahma and Mercier.

"Now I got trouble again. Dese men got toothpick shoe, long overcoat, no mackinaw, no warm shirt, no mitt, no cap. What I'm goin' to do wit' dam. Dey no real man, dose city dudes. Dey smoke pimp sticks, paper pipe (handrolled cigarettes) all de time."

"Well," advised Mercier, "you go to our company store and get the men fit clothes for the woods. Get them underwear, mackinaws, wool socks, wool mittens, shoes, rubbers, anything they need. But take away their city clothes until the spring breakup, so they won't run out on you. The company will give you credit for whatever you buy, just so you get the logs out."

WHEN PINE WAS KING

The city dudes stayed in the camp all winter and did a fair job of getting out the stuff. When they left for Milwaukee Ed deducted the cost of their woods outfits and returned their city clothes.

Uncle Tellas worked in the camps in winter but spent his springs, summer and fall at leisure in town. An ardent Catholic, he always worked for the church. The priest rounded up some volunteers one summer to mow the grass and straighten up the gravestones in the dilapidated church cemetery. Uncle Tellas reluctantly agreed to assist.

As the sun grew hotter the men loafed in the shade of a tree. The good Father became restless, fearing that the work would not be completed that day at the rate the men were working.

"Men, we want to get this all done today. We'll have to get a move on."

"By the Holy Jesus, Father," replied Uncle Tellas, "If you want to get this all done today, you'll have to get more God damn help."

Tellas dug in and in lifting a monument that was tilted over, he strained himself and his hernia came down. The priest rushed him to the local hospital where the doctor told him to take off his clothes and get in bed. He took off his greasy overalls and shoes and crawled into bed with his long-handled red underwear on. The nurse on the case came into the room and noticed the dirty sleeves of his underwear showing from under the blanket. She told him he would have to remove all of his clothes for the operation. He rebelled and yelled in a voice that reached the full length of the long corridor:—

"By Cris, you know me only a few minutes and already you are damned familiar."

The nurse summoned the doctor but still Uncle Tellas refused to remove his underwear. The doctor gave him a hypodermic to put him to sleep in order to remove his underwear.

After the operation Uncle Tellas was too weak to get out of bed to go to the toilet. He refused to let the nurse bring him a bedpan. He would hold back as long as he was able—then disaster! But by the time they had him housebroken he was ready to leave the hospital.

Mike Keegan came over from Ireland and worked in a local mill. A bachelor, he had few restraints placed upon him. Wages were good and he went on a toot every pay day. However, he saved money and bought government bonds. He was a faithful workman and loyal to his employers. Saving, except for occasional sprees, he was thrifty of his employer's equipment. When electric lights were installed in the mill, it was Mike's duty to turn the lights off and on and to replace the burned-out bulbs. These latter he saved until he had a burlap sack full. He took the sack of bulbs to his boss and asked him to take them to town to have them refilled.

Mike decided he would return for a brief visit with the folks in Ireland. Each payday he placed an amount in a special travel fund. The boat trip over was a rough one. A great storm came up and he became deathly seasick. Rather than face another such experience he decided to stay in Ireland the rest of his life.

One day months later a local banker asked Mike's former employer what had happened to Mike. He had left between $8000.00 and $10,000.00 in government bonds lying in the bank vault for safekeeping. Mike had thought he was merely donating his money to the "guv'ment". The money was sent to him and he lived in luxury in Ireland for several decades.

CHAPTER EIGHT
When Men Were Men

Jim Murphy, whose feats as a timber cruiser, drive foreman and lumber camp boss, were extolled in my volume, "Between the Iron and the Pine," was one of the men whose mark was left on the big pine era of the U.P. As a sturdy Irish lad he left his native land to seek his fortune at Perth, Ontario. Now a man of 75, he lives in a two room shack beside the track of the Chicago, Northwestern Railroad, where once stood the thriving settlement of Elmwood in Iron County, where the only industry now is the crossing of a county road and a railroad track. Jim's ambition for a fortune was never reached, yet today he looks back on a life filled with adventure, struggle, excitement and satisfaction in the days when men faced nature at its fiercest and finest.

Jim's first job was driving a team hauling supplies to lumber camp twenty-five miles from town. He made the trip from the camp to town with an empty sleigh in one day and in two days returned with a load of beef, pork, flour, sugar and other supplies used in the camps. When the spring breakup came the married men went home for the summer and the single men remained in camp waiting for the spring log drive down the swollen river. The idle men undertook to make enough maple syrup to add flavor to their meals during the grueling work on the river. They lacked the usual big iron kettle used for boiling down the sap.

Louie LaPointe, the camp foreman, sent Jim to another camp to get the kettle on the two horse sleigh. On the return trip half way from the main camp he drove his team over a three mile lake on the ice. When he was half way across he heard the howl of a pack of wolves. His horses picked up their ears and started off at a fast walk. As he looked around Jim saw wolves appearing from the woods around the lake and coming toward him. Gradually the pack closed around the team and man The horse set off at a run. As they gathered momentum, Jim knew he could not control the frightened horses. He had a pair of fine horses and he wanted to save them. Tying the reins to the sleigh box, he fastened a hand ax in his belt and slid the four foot iron kettle off the sleigh onto the ice. He dropped off the sleigh and let the horses gallop off to the camp. The wolves followed the team to the edge of the woods, then returned to inspect the kettle and Jim. He raised the kettle and crawled under as the wolves reached it. Within seconds the wolves were digging around the kettle to get at their victim. As paws appeared under the edge, Jim used his ax to chop them off. Blood streamed under the kettle but as each casualty withdrew other paws dug in. This continued until daylight reflected from the ice. Suddenly the howling of the wolves stopped. Chains clanked and voices came near. Strong hands lifted the kettle off and Jim breathed fresh air again.

The team had reached the stables and the men at the camp heard the ringing of their harness bells. The foreman and two men set out to find their missing supply teamster. Bloody tracks led to the woods and missing paws dotted the ice.

Jim's first river drive was down the Brule River between Michigan and Wisconsin. When the last log went over the falls into the Menominee River, the river hogs received their pay checks and headed for Florence, Wisconsin, one of the tough spots in that area. At the edge of the village Mina Mudge had a big dance hall, bar and a bunch of "girls" for the entertainment of the liquor hungry men. It didn't take long for the river men to shed themselves of their hard earned dollars. There were a dozen or more saloons and three or four sporting houses. Mina's mother ran one of the latter and her father played the fiddle and called off the dances in the hall. When fall came her father packed his grip, put his Bible under his arm and went south, where he preached the gospel to the heathen during the winter. The next camp breakup found him back at his old stand helping to mulch the drunken drivers of their cash and virtue.

Jim stated that you could see a fight at anytime either in a saloon or on the dirt street or wooden sidewalks. Jack McHugh had a fight one day but had too much firewater under his belt and lost. He went to bed to sleep it off. Jim went to see him the next morning. Jack asked him to get him some whiskey. Jim got him a beer glass full and Jack drank it all, pulled on his shoes and went looking for his man again. When he met him he yelled:—

"We'll go out on the green where the bull gets his breakfast and try it over again."

This time Jack won the rough and tumble, but neither was seriously maimed.

The McDonald boys of Menominee were a tough crowd who ran the town. One night they got into a saloon fight and killed a halfbreed Indian. The officers arrested them and placed them in the little town jail. Every lumberjack who had been beaten up by the McDonalds gathered for a lynching. The mob battered down the jail door and cell with a railroad tie, tied ropes around the two brothers, hitched the rope to a wagon and dragged them down the street. Some of the jacks jumped upon their bodies to ride them. Jim said that not one man who had a hand in the lynching died a natural death.

Jack Farrell was superintendent at a camp near Watersmeet and drove a spanking team of bronchos on a buckboard. As he passed a gravel pit he saw a man's feet sticking out of the sand. The authorities dug a hole beside the body and rolled it out of its grave. He had been beaten and robbed. His boots and socks had been stolen and his money taken. His identity remained unknown and the place was named Dead Man's Hill.

The last summer Jim worked at the camp near Watersmeet, he was sent to Camp 7 to drive the last of the logs down to the mill. The cook had gone to town on an extended spree after his long winter of abstinence. The cookee volunteered to do the cooking. He wanted flour. They gave him some. One Sunday as the men were lying on the grass resting from a rough week in the river, the cookee made a batch of bread. It came up fine when he looked at it. He came to the door and called to Paddy Costigan to come see it.

"They said I couldn't bake. I'll show you."

When he opened the oven door, his bread was down flat.

Paddy turned to him:—

"You better put a Jackscrew under the stove or that bread will take the bottom right out of her!"

The poor boy wasn't a cook but he was a damn good hornblower!

The worst fight Jim ever witnessed occured at Camp 7. Jack McConnell and Tom Davis had rubbed each other the wrong way on several occasions. They were both powerful men with no spare fat on either. They were rivals at loading logs, telling stories in the bunkhouse at night and both heavy drinkers in town. One Sunday morning Davis was washing his clothes in the camp boiler when McConnell came by and brushed against him not too gently upsetting the boiler and hot water. Davis called McConnell a dirty bum. McConnell swung a haymaker and knocked his opponent to the dirt. Davis got to his feet and directed a kick with his heavy boot at McConnell's chin. McConnell caught the boot, twisted it and flung Davis to the ground again. Slowly, Davis got to his feet and with a bellow like a bull dove at McConnell's middle. Both men went down in a heap and the dust flew head high as they struggled to get a hold on each other's throat. Sixty men barged out of the bunkhouse and made a circle. The men fought on the ground and on their feet. McConnell's right eye closed from a savage blow and Davis' nose bled like that of a stuck hog. They fought for an hour. Fists struck faces with sickening thuds. Both men were so exhausted that they could barely raise their arms to strike. They were black from the dirt in which they rolled. Neither appeared to have acquired an advantage when Dan Shay, the boss, stepped between them and ordered them to stop. Both men were dripping blood. Shay took them to the horse watering trough and sloshed them down with pails of cold water, then ordered them into their bunks.

Jim tells of working with a crew putting up snow fence one fall when their discussion turned to religion. One of the men started to criticize the Catholic Church, its priests and nuns. Jim stood the abuse as long as he was able, then told the man that since the priests and nuns had no one to defend them, he would take on their cause. The men immediately made a ring around the two men and the battle was on. Hammer fists flew and met their marks. Bone thudded against bone. Blood spurted. The men cursed. Jim said of the result:—

"If you got into trouble on that job the foreman had to fire you. But I stopped that Klu Kluxer from running down anybody for their religion. I got fired all right and spent a long time in St. Mary's Hospital at Marquette. But I was a hero to those Sisters. If I had been a millionaire, I couldn't get better care than I got from the doctors and the Sisters. I've got all the respect in the world for the Sisters and couldn't stand for anyone telling lies about them. I don't ever want to hear anybody's religion run down. We are all trying to get to the same place."

Beechwood was another small settlement in the pine woods near Elmwood where Jim Murphy lived and worked. A Swede named Israelson lived on a small farm in the Beechwood area. He had a nice, respectable wife but no children. He was a queer fellow and went on terrible tears of temper, driving his wife out of the house and abusing his cattle. His wife's mother and father came to visit them with their horse and buggy. The father stopped at the gate to let his wife out of the buggy, then

SKIDDING LOGS

This teamster and horses drew logs on travois from the cuttings to the skidways where the logs were piled, awaiting the hauling by bunked sleighs.

Michigan Historical Collection

PLOWING OUT THE ROAD

Five and six teams of horses drew the great snowplow to clear snow from hauling roads.
Burton Historical Collection

THE WORLD'S FAIR LOAD

This load of pine was decked in Ontonagon country, hauled to the river, then loaded on flatcars and shipped to the Chicago World's Fair where it was reloaded on sleighs and exhibited.
Burton Historical Collection.

ON THE SKIDWAY

These lumberjacks with their canthooks and horses decked logs on the riverbank rollways awaiting the "breakup" and the river drive.

Michigan Historical Collection

drove into old man Greenland's yard across the road to water his horse. The wife walked to her daughter's house and as she stepped onto the porch her son-in-law went beserk and shot her with his deer rifle. Then he drew a bead on the father-in-law and the horse and shot them both. Greenland was plowing on top of the hill north of his house and Israelson's shots missed him by inches. Greenland dropped his reins and took for the tall timber.

Two lumberjacks came down the road and Israelson shot at them but the distance was too great. They, too, took off through the woods. Mrs. Israelson and her little sister ran across the road to Greenland's for protection. He killed both of them. Then he shot his own dog. That was all he saw moving, so he went into the root cellar where he brought out a few sticks of dynamite. He could not find the caps and fuse. As he came out of the root cellar he set the house on fire. Placing the dynamite beside his wife's body, he lay beside her and pulled the trigger of his rifle. The shot missed the dynamite but not Israelson.

Mrs. Greenland watched the carnage from her upstairs window and saw everything that happened. She stood back from the window, fearing that the madman would see her and shoot her too. Jim O'Brien, the coroner, took the five bodies with horses and wagon to Iron River for burial and stated it was the grimmest sight he had ever witnessed. The corpses were laid out in the undertaking parlors where even school children were allowed to view them. Some of the children had nightmares for weeks thereafter, according to their parents.

Charlie Saxon started to build a new house on the old foundation of the Israelson home. It was half completed

WHEN PINE WAS KING

when it was struck by lightning, and twice thereafter. Saxon had what was left of the house moved to another location. Later Tom Hoskins and his mother built a small cottage on the property close to the road. One evening as they and friends were playing cards in the cottage lightning struck the house. The Hoskins immediately moved out. A farmer nearby had two cows wander into a pasture of the Israelson farm to graze. He found one cow dead and the other very sick but he claimed the animals were hexed, not poisoned.

In the 80's and 90's, Jim Murphy explained, when the lumber companies got their camps built and started lumbering the lumberjacks never saw the camps in daylight except on Sundays until the camp broke up in the spring. Up before daylight, the men ate breakfast by kerosene lamplight, then started for the cuttings before the sun was up. Work in the woods stopped when it was too dark to use an axe. After the walk of two or three miles back to camp, darkness had again settled down. By the time the supper was over the men were ready to roll into their straw-covered bunks.

When the camp clerk figured up what you had coming for your winter's work, he would make a notation on a sheet of paper out of a tablet, deduct your van bill, your hospital ticket and your donations, which sometimes amounted to quite a lot as there wasn't a week but someone came into camp for a handout—churches, cripples, blind or just broke lumberjacks. After all these deductions the jack had little coming, especially if he had bought a suit of clothes from Fred Hartley, who made the camps to measure and take orders for clothes which would be ready when the purchaser came to town. The time slip could be cashed at a bank, grocery or saloon, but each cashier would deduct 10% for the accomodation.

Most of the jacks would owe the hotel keeper a bill from the last summer or fall and as a rule would pay this account first. Then if the saloon was not first visited he paid a month's board in advance, and bought a new hat, underwear, dress shirts, tie to go with the new suit, a pair of dress shoes and perhaps a pair of driver shoes all calked up if he were going on the spring drive. So when all these purchases were made there was little left from his average wage of $1.00 a day and board. The only fortunes that were made were made by the lumber camp owners.

Few of the lumber companies in the early days furnished fresh meat at the camps. They said it cost too much. The retail price of hindquarters of beef was five cents a pound dressed, hogs four cents, eggs $3.00 a case, butter 8 to 10 cents. Oleo was served in the place of butter. The jacks called it wagon grease. The main diet was salt pork, corned beef (red horse), beans, bread, potatoes, prunes and vinegar. An abundance of pie, cake and cookies was served if the camp was lucky enough to have a good cook.

Jim was laying out a logging road for the P. C. Fuller Company. He was assisted by a man called Zorkey as a tree blazer. Zorkey took sick in the woods and Jim brought him to town where his wife took him to the hospital. The doctor told her that he would have to operate the next day although the case was not serious and he would recover.

"Well," said the woman, " if you have to operate on him what about those monkey glands I heard about? Can you put them into him?"

"Sure," replied the doctor with a twinkle in his eye. "We'll do that for you."

The operation was performed and Zorkey recovered. A month later his wife met the doctor on the street. He asked her how her man was getting along. She replied:—

"Fine."

"By the way, how do those monkey glands work."

"That's all bunk, Doc. All he does is sit on the edge of the bed and scratch himself and holler for more peanuts."

In "Curley-headed" Johnson's camp where Jim worked one season the floors of the bunkhouse and stables were made of peeled poles with the top side adzed off so the men would not break their ankles walking on them. The poles were crooked and had wide cracks between them, so no sweeping was necessary except on Monday morning after a littered Sunday. Two roller towels were supplied for 30 men. If the supply of softsoap didn't run out, the chore boy washed the towels once a week. Everyone was lousy and full of "crabs." The jacks could not keep clean no matter how often they washed their own clothes. Boiling and kerosene relieved the situation briefly, but the vermin infested the cracks in the bunks and logs of the bunkhouse and soon found their victims. In the fall and spring wood leeches clung to the men's skins and burrowed in. Jim said you didn't have to have monkey glands to make you scratch.

Cook Brothers logged on Cook's Run, a short distance from Iron River. One March the weather broke early and it looked as though the logs would be left in the woods until another spring if they could not be gotten out within a few days. The haul to the rollway was twelve miles and the road was getting soft. The foreman put four horse teams on each load. They bought nose bags for the horses, filled them with oats so the horses could eat whenever they had the chance while loading and unloading. The crew and horses worked day and night. If a horse became exhausted, it would be unharnessed, taken out of the team and another horse taken out of the barn. The "played-out" horse would be left at the roadside to stagger back to the camp to be fed and rested up. After two days it would again be put to work hauling logs. The teamsters could snatch a meal as they passed the cook house and take a lunch with them. The logs were finally all landed on the river bank before the roads "went out."

"Haywire" Stewart used oxen only at his makeshift camp. Not being able to afford a blacksmith and the necessary equipment to shoe oxen, he drilled holes in the oxen's hooves and sewed the cleft shoes on with haywire to enable the animals to negotiate the iced roads. His oxen drivers all carried a bunch of haywire with them to replace a shoe which came loose on the haul.

CHAPTER NINE

Fleecing the Lumberjack

AFTER A LUMBERJACK had worked in the deep pine from October to April, wet to the waist at times, up to his knees in snow, freezing in below zero weather, with little or no entertainment, surrounded by other men of his own level, he was ready for what town offered him. With a stake of $150.00, more or less, minus deductions for tobacco, clothes, and whatever donations he may have made to other injured or sick jacks or to the traveling preacher, he headed for the nearest town at the spring break-up.

Lumber towns like Seney, Watersmeet, Ironwood, Hurley and Iron River were well equipped beforehand for the invasion of the hundreds of men dumped into them, ready for booze, bragging and women. The local grocers and saloon keepers had plenty of money on hand to cash the time slips which the men carried from the camps, at a ten percent discount. Liquor supplies were stacked high, extra bartenders were brought in to help quench the thirst of the liquor-hungry men. Where bawdy houses were permitted or ignored by the law fancy women came with their alluring finery, rouged lips and cheeks and cheap perfume to set up their trade in the red-curtained houses on the edge of town.

Local mothers warned their off-spring of the impending invasion and carefully shepherded their children off the streets. The local livery stables slicked up their carriages and groomed their horses to transport the men from town to town. Drygoods stores laid in a supply of suits, shirts, derby hats, Sunday shoes and socks for the men who would soon cast off their rough woods clothes for the finer habiliments of civilization.

They were ready. Let 'em come!

The stomp of heavy boots soon echoed on the plank sidewalks as the men piled off the trains, supply wagons and buggies. The more cautious and experienced men, remembering what happened last year, headed first for the grocery stores to cash their time slips and deposit all but a few dollars against the day when their money and credit would run out. A few went to the postoffice to send their families money orders, holding back a few dollars to treat the boys a round before setting off for their homes at distant parts. Some paid off their debts in the stores and saloons to establish their credit against the time when they would need clothes, tobacco or liquor "on their face."

The saloons were crowded to the doors as the men made the rounds, meeting friends and "loading up." Whiskey and beer splashed on the polished bars and onto the sawdust-covered floors as they crowded around, drinking, treating and back-slapping in their enthusiasm and leave-taking. Saloon keepers cashed time slips and stored away excess money for the jacks in safes as a reserve for leaner days. Some of this money dwindled rapidly, for when the men came back after a few days they were told that they had drank it up already. As they became unsteadier and unsteadier on their feet, they became more lavish with their treats. Whenever a jack flashed a five dollar bill it

FLEECING THE LUMBERJACK

meant a treat for the house. No change was given back. The cost was five dollars and no questions asked.

Tavern keepers made a great fuss over the men while their money lasted. They served free lunches of cheese, pretzels and rye bread at the end of the bar to keep their customers in the place. With rooming houses crowded to capacity, some of the men found lodging on the floor in the back rooms of the saloons, there to be frisked by the saloon keepers and hangers-on. Once their stake was gone, their credit came to an end. Then, unceremoniously, they were told that they were no longer welcome in the place. Sentiment had no place in a saloon for the penniless.

In one saloon in Seney a bartender kept a blackjack under the bar. When asked its purpose, he remarked:—

"Dis is me gavel. When I asks for order and don' get it, I wraps somebody over the head. Den I gets order."

As ready cash dwindled, the men drifted off to other towns or sought work in the local sawmills or on farms. Since work was scarce in the summer and operations in the woods were at a low ebb, many of the men were "on the bum," traveling from saloon to saloon seeking free drinks and free lunches. They remained "bums" until the next fall when woods foremen sought them out and shipped them back to the camps for another four or five months of back-breaking work and monotony.

Some camps had the practice of postdating the lumberjack's checks or time slips. Due in March, they were dated in April. When they were cashed before the due date the saloon keepers or banks deducted ten percent and split with the lumber companies. In one lumber town the company operated a big rooming and boarding house where the men could stay when they were not working in the camps. The men were not paid at the end of the winter season but were given credit at the boarding house. The company owned a general store where the men could use their credit slips until they worked in camp again.

This company's mill issued books of credit coupons instead of cash. Saloon keepers accepted these slips and took off their ten percent for cashing them. One saloon keeper had accumulated $600.00 in coupons when his saloon burned to the ground. He took the coupons to the mill owners to pay for lumber to rebuild. The owners at first refused to allow him to pay them in this manner but they were finally convinced by an attorney that the coupons were legal tender.

Before the men started back to the camps in the fall the saloons would sell them a bottle of whiskey on credit. Some made the rounds and hid their bottles until they had accumulated several before taking off.

At Kenton one of the saloon keepers had a unique method of keeping lumberjacks coming back to his place even in winter. Men kept drifting into that district almost daily and were shipped off to the camps along the logging railroad. When a good load of jacks boarded the train, this saloon man boarded it too with a case of whiskey in bottles which he passed out to the men before they reached their destination, telling them they could pay when they came to town again. Once having tasted whiskey in camp, they soon left camp again for Kenton and their generous friend, there to spend whatever money they may have earned. This same saloon man fleeced one jack of $80.00 one night. When his victim came around the next morning to demand his money, the saloon keeper told him he had spent it all on his friends, gave him a pair of mittens and a bottle of whiskey and sent him off on the train to camp.

At Sidnaw the social life became so intolerable that the better lumber operators of the district clubbed together and built a little jail to incarcerate the inebriates. They hired a constable who nabbed the first trouble maker to serve as an example to the others. That night the first prisoner dug his way out through the dirt floor with his hands. The good lumbermen had neglected to put a plank floor in their hoosegow.

Treatment of the men in the camps was frequently on the same level as in town. Seven young men in their late teens and unexperienced in lumber camp ethics hired out at one camp for $16.00 a month plus food and a bunk to sleep in. They did a creditable job and produced their share of sawlogs. They neither drank, smoked, or chewed. When the spring breakup came, the foremen deducted $8.00 from each of their time slips for tobacco. They complained:—

"We didn't smoke or chew. How come you charged us $8.00 for tobacco we didn't use?"

"Well, it was there to buy. It's your hard luck if you didn't buy it."

Undoubtedly the foreman received a bonus for operating his camp so economically.

A few lumber companies operated both camps and mills. Men who worked in the woods for the company merely shifted their place of employment from camp to mill in the spring and from mill to camp in the fall. Many of the companies operating in this manner also owned a town store where groceries, meat, clothing and other supplies were sold. Some of these companies required their employees to purchase all their supplies at the store. To enforce this rule, the companies issued time slips or due bills which were cashable at the store only in exchange for goods which in isolated areas were priced from ten to fifteen per cent higher than in comparable stores in similar free trade communities.

Passbooks were issued by some operators in lieu of time slips or due bills. Using these, employees were required to buy from the company stores only. Not a few companies in the early Eighties issued scrips payable only in goods at their stores, but this method was so unpopular that the companies were forced to discontinue it.

One lumber company required the lumberjacks to sign an employment agreement whereby they were forced to work for a term of months and at any labor requested by the foremen before they were paid. Work begun in the fall was not payable until the breakup in the spring. In the event the laborer quit his job before the end of his employment time twenty per cent was deducted from his time slip. The company would advance enough money to pay doctor bills but other withdrawals were charged to his account. In one case where the lumberjack requested a large amount from the company to make a payment on his home in town he was required to pay interest on the loan although he had more than that amount due him in wages.

In another case an immigrant lumberjack was killed in the woods while working for the company. His widow was docked twenty per cent because her husband had failed to complete the terms of the written contract.

In the early days it was the practice of the lumber camps to feed and bunk any lumberjack who was making

FLEECING THE LUMBERJACK

the rounds of the camps seeking work. Should a camp not require additional help, the men were provided food for the day and a bed for the night, then sent on to another camp. As competition between operators became spirited and profits began to dwindle due to stricter laws and supervision by government land offices, this practice was abandoned by some. Stray lumberjacks were no longer welcome and fed. Foreman gave strict orders to the cooks not to feed any men they could not hire.

Art Murray, a lumberjack of Mio, in the Lower Peninsula, walked to Munising in the UP to seek work where jobs were advertised. At every camp where he applied, the answer was the same:

"No work, no free chuck."

Cooks guarded the cook shacks under rigid orders. Art could not get a free bunk to sleep in, so he slept on the ground under the trees in the cold fall weather. Desperate, hungry and penniless, Art approached the cook shack of a camp to find the woman cook barring the door with her arms spread across the casing.

"Won't you give me some of the scraps you were going to throw to the camp hogs?"

"No," replied the woman. "We have strict orders not to feed any camp bums."

"By God," retorted Art. "We weren't bums when your company needed good timber men. Now they use us like begging tramps. Even a horse is treated better than we are. You feed 'em and water 'em when they don't work. If they're sick, you take care of them. When we are sick you kick us out of camp. When we are hungry, you won't feed us the swill you throw to the hogs."

Over the cook's shoulder appeared the face of a girl

who was the cook's assistant and was a former resident of Art's home town.

"Give him some food," she urged. "I know Art. He is an honest man looking for work. I'll pay for it out of my pay."

The cook grudgingly consented and Art left with a sack of food which enabled him to reach Mio and a more friendly and charitable region.

The saloons' greatest competitors were the operators of the bawdy houses. These were usually located outside the town limits or on the back streets. They were designated by a red light in the door and red curtains in the windows. Deprived of the companionship of women during the long winter season, the men were easy victims of the lures of the inmates of these notorious dives. Once inside they stayed there, drinking whiskey at $1.00 a glass, whereas saloons sold it for ten cents, and loving for so much a "throw". When they had become stupified, they were easy victims of "rolling". The women stuffed their purses with greenbacks until they bulged. A month or two of this type of fleecing sent them back to the big cities with fortunes enough to last them until the next spring.

According to John Bellaire, a clerk at the general store at Seney, one of the women brought her ill-gotten wealth to the store safe. When she was ready to leave town she withdrew over $1500.00, stating that she was going back to a small Illinois town to be married.

"Then you must be engaged to some man down there," remarked Bellaire.

"Yes," replied the woman, "We became engaged, then decided that we would separate and each make a stake before we are married. I guess I beat him to it."

FLEECING THE LUMBERJACK

The sporting houses of Seney, as in other lumber towns, were crowded with women-hungry men. In the rush days these houses could not hold all the women who flocked in to get their share of easy money. Many came in on the morning train from Marquette, did their illicit business in the stalls of the livery stables, then returned to Marquette on the midnight train, loaded with money, given by or stolen from the lumberjacks. A "night in" cost from $2.00 to $5.00. The inmates never molested the men on the streets except to parade their wares as they drove in fancy buggies around the town.

Jack Mitchell, a woods foreman, recalls:—

"And there were some good looking heifers among them."

BULLS O' THE WOODS
Early camps used great teams of oxen for skidding. These patient animals were easily handled, seldom sick and ate less, although they were slow.
Burton Historical Collection.

EARLY DAY OX TEAMS

The roundup of oxen on their way to the camps. As many as 60 oxen were used in some camps. Note bullwackers and their bull whips.

Courtesy George H. Hedquist

GIANT MICHIGAN PINE

This butt log was over six feet in diameter. Note owner's stamp at the ends.
Burton Historical Collection

HORSEPOWER IN THE LUMBER CAMP

Horsepower in the lumber camp. Foreman's trotter and sulky at left used to take him on his rounds in summer and fall. Horses received better care than the lumberjacks.

Michigan Historical Collection

CHAPTER TEN

Characters of the North

Colorful characters in early UP were legion. Men of all walks of life and background drifted into that north country,—some to look up land and timber for speculation, some to open lumber camps, to seek work in the woods, business and professional men to open services in the towns, gamblers, pimps, "fancy" women to get their share of the winter's takes, saloon keepers and just drifters and refugees from the law. A few, eschewing the towns and lumber camps, built shacks in the woods, far from other habitations and activities, to live the life of hermits and trappers. In the main they were men who had the fortitude and urge to try their hand at seeking a living and perhaps a fortune in the new and rugged land across the Straits. Perhaps no area in the mid-west contained so many interesting and colorful personages per square foot as did that land between Lake Michigan and Lake Superior.

Notorious was a local character called Tom Tuffy. As a boy he continually got into trouble by beating up youngsters half his age and size. A born coward, he was evasive and lawless in small ways as a boy.

Upon reaching manhood, he weighed over 250 pounds and lived by his wits. One day he entered a local grocery store and asked for a cardboard box in which to ship some material. The proprietor told him he would find some empty boxes in the basement and to help himself. He did. He found twelve cartons of tobacco which he placed out the basement window and took an empty box through the store. The owner missed the tobacco but thought his delivery boy had taken it to a customer. The next day a cigar store owner told the grocer of the good buy he had made from Tom who represented himself as the tobacco agent of a Chicago firm.

A traveling man was making his toilet in the washroom of a local hotel and removed his white shirt in the operation. When he turned to put on his shirt, it was missing. He reported his loss to the hotel manager who immediately suspected Tom whom he had seen enter the hotel. The salesman put on his coat and set out to find Tom. When he met him on the street, he said:—

"Take that shirt off right here on the street or I'll put a wooden one on you".

The usual coward, Tom undressed on the street.

Tom posed as a law enforcement officer during Michigan's early state prohibition days. He located a Polack who was making moonshine at his shack in the woods. Tom threatened to report him if he did not pay a fine of $300.00 on the spot. After digging up the money the moonshiner reported the incident to the prosecuting attorney who was in the pay of the moonshiners of the county for protection. Tom skipped to Florence, Wisconsin, but was brought back with extradition papers to face prosecution and to return the blackmail fee.

During Jack Dempsey's reign as the world champion boxer, Tom posed as the pugilist's trainer. He sent word to the boxing managers of Milwaukee that he was coming to their city to arrange a match with a local boxer and Dempsey. A big reception was held for Tom by the boxing fans and it was weeks thereafter that they learned of the hoax.

Tom had acquired a knowledge of medicine and medical terms. He became a drug addict and a drug peddler and spent several short terms in prison for his trade. His method of securing dope was to pose as a physician, visit a local doctor in his office to talk medicine, case the joint, then enter it at night to steal the narcotics. His knowledge of the medical jargon convinced his victims that he was a bona fide medical man.

Tuffy even went into veterinary practice with at least one good result. While he was standing in front of a store in town, he noticed a Finnish woman driving up the street with a limping horse. Tom walked into the road and stopped her.

"I'm a graduate of a veterinary college and practice in Green Bay. Your horse has a big lump on his leg. I can operate right here and it will cost you only five dollars." Taking out a pocket knife he slashed open the swollen leg, released the pus and blood, then tied up the incision with his handkerchief. He collected his fee then and there and the horse recovered.

Conductor Armstrong worked for the Chicago, Northwestern Railroad in 1887 hauling freight and logs between Watersmeet and Green Bay, Wisconsin. Lumberjacks rode in his caboose between the lumber camps and the towns. The road bed was laid over soft ground and in winter it was subject to alternate freezing and thawing, which resulted in a rolling and weaving track over which the freight train had to proceed carefully to avoid a spill on the curves.

Near the lumber village of Elmwood there was a particularly dangerous curve. High pine stumps stood along the track and the ground was boggy. On one occasion four lumberjacks were in the caboose playing smear. Conductor Armstrong came in and sat on the arm of the seat watching the game. When the train struck the curve, the caboose rolled over on its side. Jack McDonald, one of the four, had just raised his arm with a deuce of spades in his hand and yelled:—

"I've got low."

The side of the caboose struck one of the stumps as it tilted over. The stump crashed through the side of the wooden car. McDonald was crushed and killed. When the men picked him up he still had the deuce in his hand. It had proved to be the traditional hard luck card. Conductor Armstrong received an injury which resulted in a permanent stiff neck, and McDonald's Curve received a permanent name.

There was no compensation for accidents on the railroad, although the company was always subjected to damage suits, a costly procedure for lawyer's fees and court costs, even though no damages may have been awarded. However, to mollify Conductor Armstrong, the railroad officials promised him a life-time job. This was a mere gesture, for he would have had a permanent job in any event.

However, Armstrong managed to secure compensation in his own way. Travel by horse and buggy over the rough roads from the camps to town presented a rather hard method of travel, so the lumberjacks caught the daily log train to Iron River and other points south. Over the week-ends and at the beginning and the end of the winter logging season groups of lumberjacks would board the caboose over which Armstrong was presiding and would hand him fifty cents for fare. The conductor would punch out one ticket and pocket the balance. This practice went on for many months. One day a railroad "spotter" was aboard and saw what was happening. Armstrong was called on the carpet by the superintendent of the line and given a ten day layoff without pay. This happened several times. Finally Armstrong was given a complete discharge and the superintendent told him that he would see to it personally that he would never get another job on any railroad, placing him on a permanent blacklist.

Faced by this dismissal, Armstrong remarked:—

"Now, I would like to charter one of your special trains to get me to Canada where I can get another job."

He was "well-heeled" by this time.

During the panic of 1893 camps and mills shut down and men were stranded without work or means of securing food and the necessities of life. In some areas the situation was grave. A few lumber companies allowed their workmen to live in the camps and gave them ground in which to plant potatoes and other vegetables. Some camps doled out their food supplies as long as they lasted.

Faced with this prospect men were forced to turn to the woods and what food it offered. Deer were plentiful, rabbits were abundant. Lakes and streams were filled with fish. Berries, hazel nuts and mushrooms were there for the taking. So many were forced to live off the land and woods and the streams.

Game laws were just beginning to be enforced by the Michigan Game Commission. Enforcement officers were reluctant to pin game violations on needy people. But when men began to shoot and sell venison the law had to be enforced and fines levied.

Old Man Ericksen was caught skinning a deer in its red coat in June. The game warden brought him before the Justice of the Peace. Ericksen pleaded not guilty and demanded a jury trial. The Justice, sympathetic with the hard-pressed people collected six Irish "micks" for the jury, among them Barney Morgan, a free thinker and a notorious "flannel-mouth."

During the trial Ericksen innocently told the jury how he had been caught red-handed by the warden, practically confessing his guilt. The jury retired and came back within five minutes with a verdict of "not guilty."

The Justice asked:—

"How in hell could you men arrive at such a verdict. It's plain that Ericksen shot that deer out of season."

"Well, Judge," answered Barney, as foreman, "Ericksen is such a damned liar, we couldn't believe him."

Unless in their cups the men in the camps and woods were sparing with words. Should old friends see each other for the first time in months, they seldom greeted each other in the usual manner of city folks. To see them meet one would think that they had parted just a few hours ago. They took up their previous conversation where it had left off, perhaps weeks ago.

At a hunting camp in the north supper was about ready. Outside was total darkness. The snow lay deep and a blizzard was in progress. The guest in the camp was an attorney from "down below." The others were old-time natives in quest of venison for the winter. The door opened and a shacker named Jasper Carey, known locally as Jep, came in. He and the others, except the attorney, were old friends, but there was no greeting of any sort. Jep set his rifle down by the door, brushed the snow off his mackinaw, took a package of fine-cut out of his pocket, filled his mouth, then went to the stove to get warm.

After several minutes of silence Jep said to Joe Hoag:

"I took a blue jay out of your fox trap over at the fire line."

"Did you reset the trap, Jep?" asked John Briggs.

Jep said:—

"Yep."

A little later Hoag came to the attorney and whispered:—

"Invite Jep to stay with us and hunt. He's a helluva good shot. He can shoot the ears right off a running rabbit."

"Why don't you ask him yourself. I never met him."

"Aw, he won't stay unless a stranger in the camp invites him."

Jep put on his cap while the men were talking, pulled it down over his ears and picked up his rifle.

The lawyer asked him where he was going. Jep grunted:—

"Oh, I guess I have to be going on."

Upon receiving the invitation to stay from the stranger and asked to hunt with the party, Jep without a word put his rifle on the rack over the fireplace, took off his cap and sat down on a box back of the stove. In that way the invitation was accepted by the taciturn shacker.

Supper was announced. It consisted of stacks of pancakes, bacon, bacon grease, potatoes, bread, honey, coffee and cookies. Jep didn't wait for an invitation this time. He went to the table and before he sat down he reached over and without the aid of a fork removed eight pancakes from one of the stacks and placed them on his plate. Then he soaked them with bacon grease, scooped the potatoes onto his plate, took a slice of bread and covered it with honey, then began eating. He didn't use a fork, but cut the pancakes into large sections, placed his knife under a section and conducted it into his mouth. His grizzled cheeks bulged with food. He grunted and chomped like a hungry bear. He stowed away enough food for three hungry men. Then without a word he got up from the table, again packed his face with fine-cut and took his seat on the box back of the stove.

The men asked him where he had spent the previous night and he told of sleeping in a portion of an old log house. The house, he admitted, had only two walls and no roof but he had built a fire in the corner of the two walls and spent the night there. His principal problem was to get enough food and funds to purchase ammunition. Anyone furnishing him with those two was welcome to any game he shot.

As the stove and the food began to warm Jep up, he began to tell experiences which involved much imagination. His stories did not deal with hunting and fishing exploits but with large business deals which he had had in Pittsburgh, New York and other metropolitan centers he had never seen. He claimed that he had been party to many important lawsuits which involved large sums of money, and in these suits he was always successful, although he did not divulge what had become of the funds he had realized.

Jep stayed in camp throughout the hunting season and shot more than his quota of deer. When the men packed up to return home, Jep silently picked up his rifle and set off through the brush without a farewell. The men learned later that he had originally resided in the Lower Peninsula but left for the UP because it was getting "too damned civilized" "down below." However, he neglected to inform his wife of his destination. True to his habit of years, he did not even bid her farewell. It just didn't occur to him.

CHAPTER ELEVEN

The Valley Boys Meet Their Match

AFTER THE big timber in the Saginaw River Valley was cut and driven to the mills, great hordes of lumber jacks from that section gradually moved north to find new pine and employment in the dark woods across the Straits of Mackinac in the Upper Peninsula. Many of these "Valley Boys" brought with them a reputation of being able to out-saw, out-fight, out-drink and out-love anything that walked in stagged pants and hobnail shoes. Tough, reckless and fancy free, they made life a hazard in the little lumber towns. When they appeared on the streets after the spring breakup and the end of the river drives, women and children stayed indoors and local citizens stepped carefully. The wooden plank sidewalks were chewed to splinters by the sharp steel calks of their river shoes.

One spring the drive came down the river which ran past the edge of the village of Iron River. Seeing the town so near, the drivers jumped their jobs and charged into town with the peavies in hand, headed for the nearest saloons for a spree. To hell with the logs! They'll get hung up in a jam before long anyway!

As they moved from saloon to saloon they tore up the sidewalks with the peavies, piled the planks into the middle of the dirt street and set fire to them.

Tom Webb, the Irish town marshal, found himself unable to cope with the wild men from the camps. He sought his cousin, Tonic Webb, the fiercest rough and tumble fighter in those parts, and asked him if he would like to have some fun. Together they faced the incendiaries and Tom yelled:—

"You Valley Boys, put out that damn fire or I'll lick everyone of you—one at a time. If you want a gang fight, here's Tonic. He'll take you all on."

Tonic peeled off his mackinaw, flared his slit nose and extended his hamlike fists. The Valley Boys looked at him in astonishment. Then one by one they kicked the blazing planks apart and left for the river.

One of the Valley Boys, a six foot six giant, carried a $100.00 bill in his pants pocket and called for the drinks for the house in one of the Elmwood saloons. After the boys had had a few rounds he threw the bill on the bar and waited for his change. The bartender's eyes bugged out in surprise that any jack could have so much money in one piece. He could not make the change, so the Valley Boy picked up the greenback and walked out of the saloon. He repeated this in another saloon with the same results.

"Are there any other saloons around?" he asked one of his drinking pals.

"Sure. There's 'Pigface' Conley's joint up the track aways."

One of the local lumberjacks who had seen the Valley Boy's system set off at a run to inform "Pigface" of his prospective visitor. "Pigface," a crafty Irishman who had operated his emporium there for many years, went into the back room and brought out a cigar box full of silver and waited behind the bar. Soon the big lumberjack appeared, followed by a large company of men ready for the fun and free whiskey.

"Give the boys all they want," yelled the schemer with a flourish.

The boys lined up at the bar and whiskey flowed free for several rounds. When the $100.00 bill was slapped onto the bar, "Pigface" reached under the bar, counted out $83.50 in silver and heaped in on the mahogany. The big jack's eyes bulged and demanded his big bill back, saying he had smaller bills in his pocket. But the canny saloon keeper was adamant and made the jack buy several rounds more before he accepted the smaller bills for the big one.

The Valley Boy roared at "Pigface":—

"How in hell did you expect me to carry all that heavy money. If I carried it on the drive, I'd drown with it in my pockets."

No one was able to outsmart "Pigface." He had been brought up the hard ways of the lumber region and knew all the tricks. He operated his saloon on property owned by the Chicago, Northwestern Railroad Company and looked the part of a tough, rough, hard-drinking man of the frontier. A participant in innumerable fights and brawls in his younger days, his face showed the results— a bashed-in nose which spread over his broad, bloated face; his eyelids drooped down to reveal their red interior; his eyes were continually running and discharging tears down his cheeks and through his nose; his jowls hung down in bags on each side of his face. His scraggly grey mustache caught the saliva which dripped through his thick lips and his "Irish meerschaum" (clay) pipe was clamped between snagged teeth, stained brown.

"Pigface" imported "fancy women" to his place when the jacks came out of the woods in the spring and helped fleece the men in their cups. The railroad company officials were aware of the trespass on their property and the notorious establishment he was conducting. They requested him to move but his Irish blarney put them off with promises to clean up the place and run a respectable joint. No improvement was ever made. Conditions became worse and worse. Lumberjack absenteeism increased. Men returned to camp after a few days at "Pigface's" unfit for work.

Finally the lumber camp operators in the area asked the railroad company to remove "Pigface" and his menace. A railroad inspector came to investigate. "Pigface," with his usual craftiness, plied the investigator with drinks, then when the agent was stupified, shipped him off on the down train. Another inspector was sent up, warned against "Pigface's" blandishments. He refused to drink or accept any favors. On his return to the office a court order was entered to remove the trespasser from the property. When the sheriff served the papers, "Pigface," realizing that his end at Elmwood had come, called in all the hangers-on and gave them all the liquor they wanted. Elmwood was never the same, with Conley gone. When the last timber was cut and floated down the Iron River, the settlement folded up. Fire and removal of buildings left only one shack, Jim Murphy's, to mark the spot of a once wild, roaring lumber center.

CHAPTER TWELVE

Battle-Scarred Lumberjacks

It should not be thought that the old time lumberjack did nothing but wear out the brass rail with his calked shoes while he wore out his mackinaw elbows leaning on the bar. The fact is that he probably drank less liquor than did the city man who had it available twelve months of the year. Some of them were family men and while a few were tee-totalers, the needs of the little wife and the children at home was uppermost during the long months of absence in the quest of enough money to buy a piece of farm land and to build a home. Only those who spent their money spectacularly were apt to be remembered.

The lumberjack drank his liquor periodically on the average—when he got to town after the spring breakup or at the end of the drive. Because cutting and decking pine and drinking did not safely mix, no whiskey was allowed in the camp. Some did get in—that brought by a newcomer who wanted to "taper-off"; then it lasted only a few minutes as the boys gathered about to get a sniff as long as the bottle lasted.

Four or five months in the woods far from town developed a bad case of bottle fever in some of the men. It was natural that when a jack hit town he cut his wolf loose and loaded his crop with liquor. Attention was called to his drinking because when he drank he wanted the world to know about it. Being lonesome, footloose and "staked," he proceeded to get noisier than a barrel full of tomcats until he became so dangerous that the town marshal had to cut him down. The law never could tell whether he was going to fight, frolic or sing. Everything depended on the kind of booze the bartender dished out to him.

Some of that early stuff would raise a blood-blister on leather boots. It was a wonder that they could keep some of the juice corked. Three drinks would grow horns on a horse. After a dozen drinks live pink snakes began to form at the bottom of the glass. The jack would begin to wonder if the man in the white apron and the handle-bar mustache behind the bar was spitting tobacco in the barrel to make it taste pleasanter. If he had a suppressed fighting disposition he would soon be giving the town hell with the hide off and doing his best to uphold the lumberjacks' reputation for being wild and untamed.

Whiskey was his drink and he took it straight. Only greenhorns from the city needed a beer "chaser" to send it down. The first few burning sensation of the conversation fluid loosened his tongue and he would start arguing with the barkeep and the saloon habitues. A few more and he'd start talking about big log loads at his camp. A few more and the jack became the best damn swamper in the county, then in the state—aw, hell, in the whole bloody country, and he didn't give a cuss who knew it.

By this time the bartender grabbed the bottle and told the jack he had had enough. After some useless arguing, he zig-zagged off to the next saloon. Feeling his way down the plank sidewalk, he cursed the builders for making it so narrow and wavy. As he entered the next dispensary he was mad enough to fight his best friend.

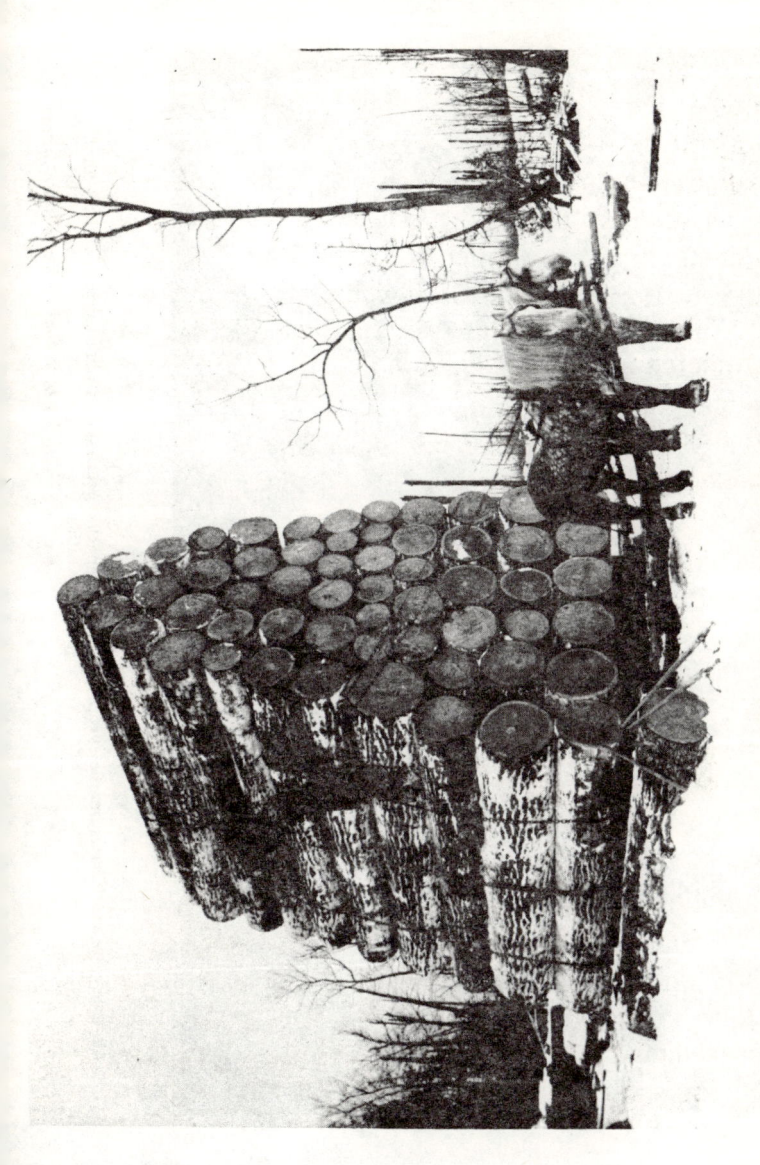

A PRIZE LOAD OF WHITE PINE

Iced roads enabled a team of horses to draw enormous loads. At times two or three teams were used to "break" the load, then quickly unhitched, and the hauling team left to complete the trip to the rollways.

Burton Historical Collection.

THE COMPANY STORE

On sale were mackinaws, maple syrup, mittens, shoepacks, peerless and plug tobacco and all lumberjack necessities.
U. of Mich. School of Natural Resources

SUNDAY IN THE MILL TOWN

Hacked out of the deep pine woods, this mill town shows the families dressed in the costumes of the Eighties, ladies in skirts, ladies in pinched waists and blooming dresses, the company store, big pine stumps and the stable and unpainted buildings.

Michigan Historical Collection

DAVID DOWNEY OF HERMANSVILLE
David Downey of Hermansville, noted timber cruiser and woods superintendent for the Wisconsin Land and Lumber Company, before the camp office.

Courtesy Mrs. Edward Hiller

Though some jacks drank when they hit town, others stayed sober enough to take the next train to their wives and families. Others took just enough to get a talking load. Their tongues would run a long time if they were well oiled. Some became tongue-tied and resorted to sign language, mumbling and gesturing unintelligibly. Should he become too belligerent and out of hand the bartender's club under the bar would put him to sleep and he would be dragged into the snake-room in the back of the saloon to sober up. When he recovered again he seldom remembered what had happened before.

The next morning his head was like a barrel, his pockets fleeced of his stake and his credit with the saloon-keeper exhausted. Then he staggered from saloon to saloon for "the hair of the dog that bit him," mooching drinks from his camp mates. Soon he became a nuisance to friend and stranger alike. With a thick tongue and an empty stomach he decided that town was no place for him. He picked up his turkey and caught the next supply team or staggered the miles back to camp to join the spring drive or work as a camp flunky for his chuck and a bunk until the camp opened for operation that fall.

CHAPTER THIRTEEN

Women in the Camps

LUMBER CAMPS were a man's world. The great majority of the lumberjacks were single with few family connections. Many came from distant parts and had few contacts with the fairer sex because of the isolation of the camps. Males in the lumber and mill towns predominated. Eligible females were married in their teens, leaving few to the choice of the bachelors.

Although many of the foremen, timekeepers, blacksmiths and other highly skilled and highly paid men in the camps were married, the wives stayed at home in town or cities, to see their husbands only after the spring break-up or the end of the log drives. A few men were privileged to have their wives in camp and lived with them in separate buildings near the operations. Occasionally the wife was employed as camp cook and her husband held some supervisory job or acted as the cook's helper or cookee.

Jack and Mrs. Mitchell lived in and around Seney where Jack was foreman for several lumber companies and Mrs. Mitchell cooked in his camps for thirty-five years. Mrs. Mitchell was a strong, fearless woman, able to handle any job or situation, be it ousting a drunken lumberjack from the cook shack or shooting a marauding bear. She arose at three o'clock to cook for from eighty to one hundred men, assisted by two cookees who washed the tin plates and mugs, scrubbed the floors and waited on the hungry men three times a day.

The breakfasts she served were typical of the early days and consisted of stacks of pancakes, fried potatoes, sausage, bacon and steaks, huge helpings of camp-made bread, cookies and doughnuts washed down with gallons of steaming hot coffee sweetened with brown sugar and condensed milk. She used a sixty pound lard can in which to raise her pancake batter.

At eleven o'clock six mornings a week Mrs. Mitchell sent out a horsedrawn sleigh with lunch to the men in the cuttings in the deep woods or the skidways. This meal usually consisted of beef stew, ham, pork, canned tomatoes, canned vegetables, beans, corn, stewed prunes, cookies and pies, with a big boiler of coffee to be heated at the fire.

Back at camp that evening supper was made of the above and extras for dessert. Mrs. Mitchell baked thirty-five or more pies a day, of cherries, apricots, dried apples, raisins and berries. She baked bread and rolls on alternate days. She cut up her own quarters of beef and whole carcasses of pork and could shoulder 100 pounds of sugar or flour and carry them from the storeroom to the kitchen.

As in all camps, the men were required to observe silence throughout the entire meal, except for a low-voiced request to pass the bacon or the potatoes. No jack was allowed to criticize Mrs. Mitchell's meals at the table, although it was their sacred right and a long established privilege to find fault with the chuck while they were in the bunkhouse or in the woods.

One dude, experiencing his first lumber camp job, got off on the wrong foot by talking of his city exploits in the cookshack. He complained that the potatoes were burned and the coffee had shoe polish in it. Although he received several kicks under the table, he kept on complaining. Mrs. Mitchell listened as long as she could stand it, then approaching the table with a long slicing knife in her hand, she asked:—

"What was that you said about the coffee, you greenhorn?"

The city fellow turned pale as he faced the irate cook, swallowed his mouthful of food and replied meekly:—

"I was just saying that the coffee had shoe polish in it, but that's just the way I like it."

One old jack had just returned from town, maudlin and unsteady on his feet, and invaded the cook shack between meals. His handlebar mustache, yellow with tobacco juice, hung below his chin. As he staggered about the place he tried to enter into a conversation with Mrs. Mitchell who ordered him out but he defied her. She was lighting her kerosene lamps in preparation of her supper. She picked up a rag, doused it with kerosene and lit it with a match. As the drunk staggered toward her, she thrust the flame under his mustache and set it on fire. He got out!

On one occasion Mrs. Mitchell's small daughter and her small dog were visiting her. They set out for a walk through the logging road with her small bore rifle. Partridge were plentiful and were a welcome change from the rugged camp diet. Mrs. Mitchell was hopeful for a few birds.

A short distance from the camp the dog bristled up his back as he looked down a deer trail, then put his tail between his legs and circled through the brush. Behind him a huge black bear rushed out and tried to follow, his nose to the ground to identify the scent. Sighting Mrs. Mitchell and the little girl the bear raised up on his hind legs and squinted at this strange sight. The cook drew a bead and carefully aimed at the bear's forehead. The first shot brought him to the ground. She calmly walked back to the camp and got two lumberjacks to haul in the beast with a pair of mules. It took two men to raise it up on a tripod for skinning. Mrs. Mitchell still has a beautiful bear robe as proof of her marksmanship.

Every lumber camp had a few hogs which fattened on the garbage from the cook shack. Sometimes it was a question as to whether the camp would eat the pigs toward spring or the bear would eat the pigs first.

Mrs. Mitchell fed two hogs one winter. They seemed like members of the family. Intelligent for pigs, they would follow the cookee when he set off with the noon lunch for the men. When they came to a narrow trail through the woods the pigs would take a shortcut to the cuttings while the cookee took the long road around. There the pigs would be waiting at the lunch fire to beg scraps from the men as they ate. When the meal was over and all the scraps had been picked the pigs would set off through the shortcut and reach the camp before the cookee arrived. The pigs were butchered when spring came and the breakup of the camp was near, but the Mitchells could not eat their pets.

One winter Mrs. Mitchell had a girl assistant who

waited on the table for her crew. One "Cute-Alex," as she called him, to attract the girl's attention, threw a cookie to another jack at the other end of the table. Mrs. Mitchell barged up and told him that there was a waitress to pass the food. Word got to Jack, the foreman-husband, who gave the jack his pay slip and said:

"Take your turkey to town. We can't have any rudeness in our camp!"

At Camp 15 of the Bay de Noc Lumber Company, a comely cook presided in the cook shack. Jake Du Fraine, the camp foreman, "took a shine to her." Daily he went into the cook shack to lean on the bread board to "soften her up," but he made no progress. He got deeper and deeper in love. She finally ordered him out of the shack. Jake went to the camp clerk and asked him to make out her time slip, meaning that she was "fired.". When Jake went into the cook shack to give her the time slip all hell broke loose. She dumped a kettle of hot bacon grease over his head, threw pots and pans at him and drove him out into the open. Jake quit his job but the comely cook stayed out the winter.

The new foreman went to the cook shack to ask her if anyone had complained about her cooking.

"Just a few," she replied. "Only nine men kicked on the chuck. That's nothing. Where I cooked last winter 100 men kicked on the chuck."

The foreman sent out for a load of supplies, among which were a bag of pancake flour and a bag of plaster pulp to be used to seal up the cracks in the cook shack. When the cook made pancakes the next morning, no one could eat them. They were hard and gritty.

"What's the matter with them pancakes?" she asked

when she saw the stacks of stiff cakes left on the plates. "That's the best pancake flour you can buy."

The foreman investigated and found that she had used the wood pulp by mistake.

"By gar," the cook retorted, "it takes a damn good cook to make pancakes with plaster."

A visitor at camp complained to the cook that her pigs back of the cook shack smelled to high heaven.

"Well, what do you suggest I do?" she asked.

"I'd either change the pigs or change the wind."

CHAPTER FOURTEEN

Buried Treasure

THE JACKSON IRON COMPANY built kilns at Fayette on the north shore of Lake Michigan to turn the hardwoods into charcoal to smelt iron ore brought down from Escanaba and the iron mines to the north and west. The owners of the company were rather straight-laced and did not allow liquor to be sold on their properties round about the operations. Whiskey was the chief cause of absenteeism at the works and as long as it was kept out profits were higher.

Blanquette, a Frenchman, made several attempts to lease or buy a spot in the community to open up a drinking place but was roughly told that he and his type of business were not wanted. He finally succeeded in buying a plot at Burnt Bluff about three and a half miles from Fayette. Immediately the complexion of the Fayette community changed. Three and a half miles was but a hop, skip and jump for thirsty men. Blanquette's became a rough place, featuring fights, drunken brawls and a sporting house in connection.

The men working in the woods and the kilns for Jackson Iron Company were the chief customers although gamblers, hard characters from the surrounding cities and pimps drifted in and made the location notorious. Families became impoverished by the free spending and the debauchery at Blanquette's. Absenteeism on Mondays made for difficulty. Wives complained to the company officials about the resulting lack of family support and the infidelity on the part of their spouses. Money was rolling in fast. Protests to Blanquette had no effect. He would retort:—

"Well, if I don't sell whiskey and run a sporting house, someone else would. I'm going to get the money while the getting is good."

Several meetings of the better element were held, backed up by indignant women of the community. As the flames of resentment grew matters got out of control. One night an unofficial vigilante committee was organized, marched to Burnt Bluff and set the saloon and bawdy house on fire.

Blanquette escaped and disappeared completely, having taken a rowboat across the bay to Escanaba. Rumor had it that he had buried his gold pieces, then the most used exchange, in the ground on his land.

Fifteen years later Blanquette faced his end in a hospital in Milwaukee. Before his death he drew a map in the presence of his physician showing where he had buried his money. The doctor was skeptical and turned the map over to his chauffer who had previously lived at Fayette.

The chauffer took a train to Escanaba and sought out Joseph Mallmann to assist him in the search for the buried treasure. At no time did he show the map but said that the money was supposed to be under a big beech tree. The agreement was a 50-50 split of what was found. Mallmann and his sons proceeded to have a local blacksmith make digging tools, shovels and steel rods with hooks and other devices for the expedition. The chauffeur, Mallmann, his sons and Mrs. Mallman set off across the bay in Mallmann's power boat loaded with food, tents, blankets and other supplies to last them for several weeks. On the way over Mallmann fell and broke his arm. On reaching shore the chauffeur and Mallmann's sons set and splinted the arm, but Mallmann, too eager to find the gold, refused to go back home.

The party camped in a tent within the stone foundation of the old saloon. They spread out the next morning and dug under every beech tree without success. The search continued for ten days. On the morning of the 11th day the chauffeur asked Mrs. Mallmann, who acted as the exploration's cook, if she would make pancakes for breakfast. She needed buttermilk and the chauffeur volunteered to get it at a farm house nearby. He set off at a fast pace over a woods trail. The family waited long past breakfast time and long into the afternoon. The chauffeur did not return. Giving up hope of finding the money or of ever seeing the chauffeur again, the family waited through the night, then set out for home in their boat.

On docking across the bay they met the captain of a coastwise boat and asked him if he had seen the missing man.

"Yes," he told them, "I saw a man of that description yesterday. He seemed to be in an awful hurry. He carried a heavy black box which he expressed at the railroad station."

Word reached Mallmann a few years later that the chauffeur had gone to his home in Milwaukee, then hurriedly left for Los Angeles where he built and operated a large garage. He turned up twice later at Burnt Bluff and did some more digging, with what success, no one was able to report. Others had feverishly dug up the entire area but no gold had been turned up. The older brother of the missing man later admitted that the chauffeur had found most of the gold.

CHAPTER FIFTEEN

Horsepower in the Camps

Horses were considered more valuable than men in the early camps. A lumberjack could be hired for $26.00 a month with "found," that is board and a bunk to sleep in. If a jack became disabled, he was sent off to town to fend for himself and another was ready and willing to take his place at the grueling work of cutting and hauling logs. When the camps broke up in the spring, the lumber company had no further responsibility for the men.

A good team of Belgian or Percheron horses cost the lumber operators from $500.00 to $700.00. They received the best of care. They were fed all they would eat of oats, hay and bran mash. Teamsters were jealous in the care of their "hayburners," as the disrespectful called them, and woe to anyone misusing them. The most skilled blacksmiths were hired to keep the horses shod with high, sharp calked shoes, which enabled them to maneuver over the iced roads and through the deep snow in the woods.

Every teamster was an amateur veterinarian and had his own favorite remedies for horse ailments—nitre of saltpetre when a horse had gotten loose in the stable and ate too many oats; pine tar smeared on a cloth-covered bridle bit for colds; lard for severe chafing from the harness and gall-cure or hemlock-water for galled shoulders and neck. Sloan's Liniment was a cure-all for cuts and bruises on horses as well as on lumberjacks.

Charlie Payne, the barn boss at Nahma for the Bay de Noc Lumber Company, had his own "receipts" for the 135 horses stabled in the huge barn on the shore of Lake Michigan. He doctored ailing horses more carefully than he would himself. He loved every hair on their thick hides.

For deep cuts, Charlie used peroxide, healing oil and a syringe.

For old sores—raw linseed oil 16 oz., olive oil 3 oz.; sulphuric acid ½ oz.; turpentine 1 oz.

For scratches—witchhazel, ague of ammonia, and glycerine in equal parts.

Tonic powder—½ oz. ginger; ¾ oz. ginseng; sulphate of iron ½ oz.; powdered allspice ½ oz.; caraway seed ¾ oz.; all ground up in a coffee mill, for use if a horse was run down.

Sores—white liniment made of 1 quart of cider vinegar, 1 pint of turpentine and 3 eggs.

While the teamster fed, groomed and watered his own team, a stable "boy," usually a retired teamster, was on duty on night shift in the stables, watching over the horses and reporting any mishap or sickness which developed overnight.

Teamsters decorated his charges out of his own pocket, with long red, white, blue or yellow horsehair tassels which hung down from the browband of the bridle or at the cross reins between the horses. Some bought bright pompoms to fasten on top of the animals' head. The horse collars were covered with wide leather housings, trimmed with shining brass medallions, to keep snow and rain from wetting the necks and chafing them raw. Celluloid rings of red, white and blue studded the harnesses and reins. A small Swiss bell hung from the bottom of the collars to warn other teamsters to turn out when a load of logs was coming down the hauling road. The music of the bells as the horses moved along was pleasant as well as useful.

At the spring breakup the teams which were not to be used on the river drives were let out to pasture on company farms, to rest up and gain weight for the next fall and winter work. Most of the horses by that time had hard callouses or galls on their shoulders from the collars and bare spots on their bodies where the harness had worn off the hair in cold weather. Galls were carefully treated with gall-cure or hardened with hemlock water. Occasionally a veterinary operated to remove the galls which did not respond to other treatment. A horse never chafed in warm weather. The cold of winter stiffened the body hair and made it brittle. These spots were rubbed with animal oil or lard to start the hair growing again. The horses fared well during their vacation on the lush grass at the farm and were ready for another season in the woods come fall. No one thought of the welfare of the lumberjack who had long since departed from the camp. He might now be in the bosom of his family, sleeping it off in the back room of a town saloon, broke, or working at a sawmill, awaiting the opening of the lumber camps in the fall. The horses had no problem of securing food and a place to rest. The lumber companies took care of that.

Oxen were used as "horsepower" in many of the camps in the early days. Two oxen weighing from 1200 pounds to a ton each, hitched in a yoke, were more powerful than a team of horses of the same weight. In deep snow they worked more easily and efficiently than horses. They never became excited or panicy. They moved at a provokingly slow gait. Their equipment was simple and inexpensive. Their yoke could be made by a blacksmith or wood worker at camp. This was placed over their necks in front of the shoulder and secured by means of an oxbow under the neck. A chain was fastened to a ring in the yoke between the animals and extended several feet behind them. This chain was then hitched around the end of a log for skidding the timber through the woods to the skidway or roadside. This contrivance, unlike a horse harness, had no whiffle trees or eveners to be caught in narrow openings between trees or stumps.

Oxen required less care, lived on less feed and were seldom subject to illness or accident. Their thick hides protected them against cuts and bruises. Their cloven hooves were shod with iron shoes, one on each cleft, giving them easy traction on snow or ice. They seldom calked each other with their sharp shoes, as was often the case with horses stumbling around in the deep snow.

When lunch time came in the woods and the men quit work to eat, the oxen knew it was time to stop too. They would stop in their tracks even though they were hitched to a log to be drawn to the skidway. No amount of persuasion by command or whip could force them to move until they were unhitched and driven to their feed.

The bullwacker or oxteam driver, needed to know the way of oxen, for he used no reins to guide them, only his voice. The command "Gee" meant to turn right. "Haw" was left. "Giddap" was go ahead. "Back" was back up. He controlled them by shouted commands and a picturesqe vocabulary of oaths, the intensity of which communicated itself to the oxen. He carried a long bullwhip with

THE COOK SHACK
In these crude log buildings great meals of hardy food were fed to the crew which was required to observe silence throughout the meal. This French-Canadian cook and his "cookee" were important factors to a satisfied gang of lumberjacks.
Michigan Historical Collection

SILENCE IN THE COOK SHACK
The men were required to observe silence. Their food was ample but coarse. The crew "ate to live and lived to eat."
Burton Historical Collection

EVENING IN THE BUNKHOUSE

This rare interior view of the bunkhouse is an accurate picture of the sleeping quarters for the men. Note the bunks on the sides, the washtub, socks hanging over the stove, the camp fiddler and the timekeeper with his record book.

Michigan Historical Collection

THE CAMP OFFICIALS
The camp foremen, clerks and scalers occupied separate quarters and were the elite members of the crew. There were no carpets or rocking chairs in the bunkhouse.
Burton Historical Collection.

THE SLASHING
Small trees were slashed down to make posts and stovewood, leaving an ideal path for destructive fires.
U. of Mich. School of Natural Resources

a swivel handle, the lash of which reached the oxen from a distance of twelve or sixteen feet. A cracker at the end of the lash in the hands of an expert bullwacker gave off a report like a twelve gauge shotgun. The driver could cut off the hair of an ox with a flip of his wrist.

In camps where both oxen and horses were used, the oxen were often sent ahead of a team of horses to tread a path through deep snow where horses would flounder. Some camps had as many as 60 head of oxen used principally for skidding logs out of the woods to decking piles, from which horses hauled the logs on great sleighs over iced roads to the rollways on the river bank.

In the late Nineties horses began to replace the slow moving oxen, which, when their days in the logging camps were over, were fattened and shipped as prime beef to the packing plants at Green Bay, Milwaukee or Chicago. Many unsuspecting meat eaters ate oxen which once skidded logs that had gone into the building of their homes.

CHAPTER SIXTEEN

The Pegleg Moocher

Gus Weasel spent his younger days as a handyman and cookee in the Sawyer-Goodman Lumber Company camps on the Brule River near the Wisconsin line. As long as he worked in the deep woods and away from the smell of whiskey, he was a faithful employee, even though it took him twice as long as the average lumberjack to do a job. If there was any liquor in the camp Gus would smell it out and steal it while the men were working in the woods. The foremen knew it meant he would be short a hand when that happened, so Gus was paid the lowest wages in camp. Should the boss relax his vigil, his handyman would hitch a ride to town on the supply sleigh and stay on a protracted spree until his money and credit ran out and he would be kicked out of the saloons.

After one of these binges, Gus returned to camp to find that the handyman's job had been filled by a younger and more dependable man. He was assigned to the job of road monkey where he was required to use an axe to clear brush off the skidding trails. Unsteady and unnerved from his diet of rotgut, he was unfit for this dangerous work. As he swung at a small sapling, his axe glanced back from the frozen wood and cut his left leg half in two.

At the town hospital gangrene set in and his weakened condition made amputation necessary. After weeks in the hospital Gus came out wearing a crude wooden pegleg. Still weak and with no income he spent his days in the only place where he found warmth and a bit of sociability—in the many sawdust floor-covered saloons. He slept where he could and ate the free lunches offered at the end of the bars. Gradually he sunk lower and lower, continually saturated with poor whiskey and feeding on the free handouts.

One day Gus appeared in Dr. Vilas' drug store with a five gallon glass jug containing three gallons of water and asked for two gallons of alcohol, explaining:—

"I just came from Emil Ammerman's drug store in Iron River and bought the last three gallons of alcohol he had. I got a job as barn boss at Sawyer-Goodman's camp. One of the horses got badly burned and we need a lot of alcohol to fix him up."

Dr. Vilas filled the jug with two gallons of alcohol and asked for his money. Gus said:—

"You'll have to charge it until I get back from camp."

The Doctor refused to allow the notorious moocher credit. Gus was in tears.

"Whoever saw such a damned stingy man who refuses to help out a poor sick work horse? Keep your damned alcohol. Pour your two gallons back in your barrel."

Dr. Vilas poured the liquid back into the barrel and handed the jug back to Gus, who cradled the diluted alcohol in his arms and departed to the back of Boynton's livery stable where he consumed the contents in a two day spree, the druggist none the wiser for the trick the old pegleg moocher played on him.

CHAPTER SEVENTEEN

Sam Jacobs-Lumber Camp Jeweler

JIM MURPHY, veteran lumber camp foreman and timber cruiser, stated that hardly a week passed in the camps that outside visitors did not come to sell watches, jewelry, hospital tickets or ask for donations for some church or welfare cause. Preachers held services on Sundays in the cook shacks; Sisters of Mercy passed subscription lists; friends of injured or sick lumberjacks asked for help for their stricken comrades. Out of their meager wages the men gave, from five cents to a quarter. Purchases and contributions by the jacks were charged against their accounts and deducted from their pay slips at the spring breakup.

One of the most successful jewelry peddlers was Sam Jacobs, an immigrant from Lebanon. Sam was a keen and rugged individual who started with nothing but the clothes on his back, finding work as he could. With a few dollars in his pocket, he started a saloon at Crystal Falls. Here he operated until he saw a man killed in a fight in his establishment.

Four Finnish miners came into the saloon and started a round of treats. In their liquified exhuberance the men at the bar began to push, knocking one of the Finns onto the sawdust covered floor. The Finn left and came back with ten other countrymen and started to clean out the place. One Finn picked up a stove poker and struck one of the pushers over the head. Sam came around the bar and ordered all of the occupants outdoors. The fighting continued in the street. Another miner was struck over the head and staggered into Sam's place and dropped dead. Sam had seen enough. He closed up his business and decided to try his hand at something more respectable, for, he said, he thought too much of his motherless son, an only child.

Sam opened a jewelry store with his brother and made the rounds of the lumber camps to sell his wares. A friendly man, he stood in well with the foremen and owners and was usually invited to sleep and eat at the camps. He had sole right to enter the camps of the Bonifas Lumber Company, the VonPlaten-Fox, the G. W. Wells and Sawyer-Goodman Companies.

When the jacks were sitting around in the bunkhouse Sam spread out his wares and sold watches, watch chains, rings, bracelets and other trinkets and took watches to be repaired at his shop. By 1920 he had enough money to start a jewelry shop of his own in Iron Mountain, a thriving lumber mill and mining town.

Sam tells of one sale he made to a Cousin Jack 'Enry, who on his arrival from Cornwall, England, coveted the ownership of a timepiece. He could not tell time but proudly showed his watch and chain. His friend, John, didn't know how to tell time either. John asked 'Enry what time it was.

"'Ere she is," said 'Enry, proudly holding up his watch.
"I'll be damned if she isn't," cried John.

Sam loved hunting and fishing. On a deer hunting trip he was accompanied by Dr. Frank Noyes of Crystal

Falls, Joe Green of Green Bay, Wisconsin and three Milwaukee men near the Bonifas camps at Watersmeet. The men hired a team and wagon to take them to the hunting camp. Jim Tucker, a Milwaukee druggist with the party, a timid man, was fearful of being lost in the woods. He brought along gummed pharmacy labels which he stuck on the trees as they went along the lumber camp road. At the hunting camp he stayed close by, going only to the pump and the outhouse, while the others roamed the woods in quest for deer.

One day Sam induced Tucker to go with him on a hunt.

"I know there is an outlaw living in the woods around here," cautioned Sam. "But I know him and I'll protect you if we meet him."

As they walked through the woods, Tucker pasted the labels on the trees, so he could find his way back. Coming to a dense thicket of pine and hardwoods, Sam pretended that he was lost. They were only a few rods from their hunting camp.

"We won't be lost long. I'll shoot twice and the boys will come out to find us," explained Sam.

"But won't the outlaw hear it and come first?"

"Well, mebbe so, but you hold your gun ready and shoot first."

Sam shot twice with his rifle, then threaded his way circuitously to the camp. Tucker in his fear did not recognize the camp.

"Here's where he lives. You stand right here with your rifle. I'll go in and shoot him if he makes a false move. If he gets me first, you plug him when he comes out."

Sam entered the cabin, winked at the men inside and shot twice into the logs, then yelled:—

"I got him!"

Tucker took off and ran two miles without stopping. Sam trailed him but could not catch up with him. Tucker reached the farm where they had hired the team and wagon and related the tale to the farmer just as Sam appeared. The farmer started to explain that there was no outlaw loose, but Sam stopped him with a finger to his lips.

"I tell you, Tucker, I shot him. There is no danger now."

The druggist was exhausted and insisted that he pay the farmer $10.00 to take them back to the hunting camp with his horses and wagon.

When they entered the cabin the other hunters were seated around the table playing poker. Not a word was spoken. Tucker looked wildly from man to man but none of them looked up or talked. There was no corpse on the floor nor any blood stains.

Finally Tucker turned to Sam and said:—

"You bloody liar. I have a notion to get the police and put you in jail or shoot you right here."

But he settled by giving Sam a bottle of whiskey which the men soon emptied with toasts to the dead outlaw.

Ice had formed on the lake near Sam's camp. As the hunters were preparing their hunting gear one morning they heard a pack of wolves howling in the nearby woods. The men rushed out with their guns to see a doe dashing out of the trees and trying to make her escape over the ice. The thin layer of ice kept breaking through and her head disappeared in the water, to come to the surface again as she struggled to find a firm footing.

The hunters let off a volley of shots at the wolves which came to the edge of the woods, then vanished. Sam and the men righted a boat which lay on the shore and with a set of old oars set out to rescue the struggling deer. By the time they reached her through the slivered ice, she was in the middle of the lake. They threw a rope around her neck and pulled her to land.

Sam ran to the cabin and brought out blankets which he threw over her and a bottle of whiskey which they poured down her throat. She was so completely weakened by fear, exhaustion and exposure that no one expected her to survive. The whiskey had the additional effect of stupifying her. The men rubbed her legs and body until she showed some signs of life again.

Rolling the animal in a blanket, they carefully carried her into the log cabin and placed her before the open fireplace. Sam brought out a Coleman heat lamp and applied it around her sides. Within half an hour she began to recover but it was three hours before she began to move her legs and raise her head. The men forgot the hunt and remained to give first aid as they knew it to apply to a deer.

By mid-afternoon some of the men left for a circuit through the woods with their rifles. Sam would take care of the doe and let her out of the cabin when she had regained her strength. He carried her into the kitchen where the cookstove was operating well with hard maple wood and laid her on the linoleum-covered floor. The warmth soon revived her and she tried to stand on her feet. At each try she slipped down again. She became panicky. And a wild deer on a linoleum floor inside a cabin was something no one had ever experienced, much less Sam. He was no wild animal trainer. The wildest animal he had ever encountered was a whiskey-loaded lumberjack.

Finally, regaining her feet the doe made a desperate spring for an open window. Sam made a flying tackle and brought her down. He yelled for help. One of the hunters in the nearby woods heard his call and rushed to the rescue, shooting off his gun twice to bring in the other nimrods. By the time they all reached the cabin and saw the situation, the doe had struck Sam in the stomach with her sharp hooves, tore his clothes to shreds and cut a gash in his right hand. But he hung onto the deer's hindquarters until help reached him.

The stovepipe was knocked down in the melee and smoke poured into the kitchen. Kettles, water pails and furniture went flying in all directions. Four men laid their hands on the deer and shoved her roughly through the open door. She went out, but just a few feet, then turned back and dashed into the cabin again. Strong again with fear, she jumped into one of the sleeping bunks and raced back and forth over the mattress and tore it to ribbons with her sharp feet. By sheer strength of numbers the men grabbed the deer by the ears, legs and body and shoved her out of the door and slammed it shut. The doe took off with a bound and disappeared into the woods, shaking her head and making the snow fly with her heels.

The kitchen and cabin were in shambles. The pot of stew was on the floor. The window was broken. Kitchen ware was dented and strewn about. The men set about to clean up the cabin and get supper, when they heard a call from Sam:

"Where's that damned Sloan's Liniment?"

"Who do you want it for, Sam? You or the doe?"

CHAPTER EIGHTEEN

The Country Doctor

During the early days in the UP the hardships of the country doctor were far greater than the monetary rewards. In rain and snow and sub-zero weather the good doctor, with his horse and buggy, managed to make his daily calls. At times the deep snow required him to use snowshoes to trek across the fields and through the woods to reach an isolated family or lumberjack in distress. Often the kitchen served as the operating room, the soup kettle as the sterilizer, and even a snow bank helped refrigerate the drugs until needed. It was he who fought for better hospital facilities in the little communities and through his diligence hospitals and clinics were erected and staffed. The country doctor was the pioneer of rural institutional care.

It would be interesting to know how many of our successful men and women of prominence were brought into the world by the men of medicine who lived in the little communities, how many operations they performed and the number of babies who received their first spankings at the good men's hands.

Dr. Robert Sturgeon of Iron River, the second physician in the village, came to the community directly out of medical school. He was born in England of a refined family and dedicated himself to the service of needy people during his medical training. Without the means of buying the usual horse and buggy or cutter, he made his way to his patients by bicycle, the first vehicle of its kind in that country of rutted roads and cowpaths. When winter came and the roads and paths were slippery with ice and snow, the good man would bandage cotton strips around the tires to prevent slipping.

As was usual in these isolated communities where boom and depressions came along with the ups and downs of the market for lumber and iron ore, the doctor's bills were the last to be paid. Often the payment was made in the form of farm produce, chickens, beef and pork.

But snow, sleet, rain or tornado deterred not this young man of medicine. His office and treatment room were scantily supplied with drugs and surgical instruments. Medicine was rather in its infancy. Far removed from the big hospitals and clinics of the large cities, Dr. Sturgeon was completely on his own.

In 1895 Vera Peterson, aged seven, lived with her parents and brothers and sisters in a little log house in Stambaugh township, five miles from Iron River. Her mother had brought in a tubful of snow to melt for the children's bath and had gone to the barn to milk her cow. Vera and her little brother were frolicking in the snow before the kitchen stove. A spark flew from the wood stove onto Vera's woolen dress. The flames blazed up into her face. Mrs. Peterson came into the house with a neighbor woman to see her daughter ablaze. She threw a blanket over the child and wrapped her in it to smother the fire. She immediately sent the neighbor to the school, which her son, Peter, was attending, and to direct him to run to his father who was working in the woods two miles away.

THE COUNTRY DOCTOR

The father ran the two miles to the farm, hitched up the horse and drove madly the five miles to Iron River for Dr. Sturgeon, who came back with him. The little doctor treated the girl but did not think she would live long, due to the third degree burns over her back, hips and legs. Daily thereafter the doctor called at the home by horse and buggy, for two weeks, then at two and three day intervals.

Vera lived through the crisis period somehow. A great skin grafting was now necessary. The doctor sent word to the neighbors through the farming country to come to the Peterson home to offer skin from their bodies. When that supply was exhausted, Dr. Sturgeon engaged the Boynton Hotel horse-drawn bus to haul adults from Iron River to the Peterson home for additional grafts. Between 75 and 80 individuals gave squares of skin for Vera. Pieces of skin half an inch square were cut from each individual, then each piece was cut in fours and spotted around the burned areas. The grafting took place over the period of over a month until Vera was able to travel in the farm wagon over the rutted roads to the doctor's office and treated for over a year.

The Boynton Hotel donated its bus for the many trips. When Peterson asked for the doctor's bill, he was told it amounted to $75.00.

No history of the early lumbering days would be complete without mention of the services performed by the medical men. No call for aid or help was ever denied. No thought was given to the hardships endured on the long, hard, cold trips that were made to reach the patient suffering from some woods accident, to render first aid, then assist in the removal of the injured to the villages where they could be more properly cared for and restored to health and usefulness.

Dr. Frank P. Bohn was born on an Indiana farm and had graduated from medical school which offered a two year course, then considered enough to serve the rather elemental needs of the time. A request came to the school for a young physician at the lumber town of Seney where there would be abundant opportunity for practice but little in the way of income. He arrived in Seney in July of 1890.

One of Doctor Bohn's first calls was to a lumber camp forty-five miles from Seney. A young man working at the camp had his leg crushed by a rolling log. He could not be hauled on a sleigh over the rough trails, so a messenger was dispatched for Dr. Bohn. He hastily packed his black bag, saddled a horse and rode to the village of Grand Marias, a distance of over thirty miles. There a boat took him to the mouth of Sucker River twelve miles east. A team of horses and a jumper hauled him to the camp with the doctor walking most of the way as the "springs" of that rough craft were none too limber. By this time it was a question as to who needed treatment most, the accident victim or the victim of the long journey. He treated the injured logger, gave orders as to his further care, then started back on his long, rough journey to Seney, over ninety-six miles round trip. The doctor's pay was fifty dollars from the lumber company. The patient lived to become the father, grandfather and great-grandfather of a great brood of children.

Another casualty was a strapping young six foot jack who was a top decker at Dan Hough's camp eighteen miles northwest of Seney. As the cross haul team pulled a big

CAMPS IN THE ROUGH

Lumber Camps were rough and crude structures for temporary use. Note the tarpaper roofs, icicles, and blankets being aired.

Courtesy George H. Hedquist

SUNDAY IN CAMP

Women visitors came only on Sundays when the men spent their time at washing, "crumb-picking," playing cards and telling "whoppers." Note cook in white apron, the "cookee" with the dinner horn and the men dressed in their Sunday best.

Michigan Historical Collection

A "HAYWIRE" OUTFIT

Small operators, working "on a shoestring," were dubbed "haywire outfits" because their equipment was castoffs and often repaired with baling wire.

Burton Historical Collection

WOODS RECLUSE

John The Bull and his trained team of bulls. Unusual harness with horse collars turned upside down, bulls tied together and traces and whiffle trees and eveners.

Courtesy George H. Hedquist

log to the top of the rollway the chain broke and the log crashed on top of him. The men sending up the log saw the accident and were confident that he had met his death. Fire flew from his eyes and an unmerciful moan escaped his lips. The horses standing below began to whinnie, sensing that something unusual had happened. The young man was carried a mile to camp and Dr. Bohn was sent for. He arrived by horse and cutter that evening and rendered what first aid he could.

The next morning the doctor returned to the camp by log train twelve miles and walked six. A stretcher of poles and camp blankets was made, the young man laid upon it and carried the six miles to the railroad siding. Hough sent along twelve sturdy lumberjacks to help, with the doctor following to administer opiates along the way. The victim was placed in a box car and the men held the stretcher off the floor the twelve miles to Seney to ease the jar of the car. The man was in terrible pain and not even the doctor expected him to live. He was placed in a room in the "Whitehouse Hotel" in the absence of a hospital where he lay for three weeks. When he showed signs of recovery, Dr. Bohn improvised a stretcher which enabled him to encase the body in a plaster of paris cast. When this was accomplished, the young lumberjack remarked with a smile:—

"Well, boys, this is the first time I was ever in Paris."

Dr. Bohn made few second calls upon his patients in the woods unless they were specifically requested. The injured and ill were left in the hands of their friends. The doctor recalled no cases of infection. He mended broken limbs, stitched severed tissue and attended cases in surroundings which would make a modern practitioner shudder. Perhaps it was the type of individual who made up the population and the kind of life they led that made recovery possible. Perhaps it was that these individuals, so positive, so assertive and so colorful made the difference.

CHAPTER NINETEEN

The Cropped Ear

JOEL WATERS was always an interesting pioneer. The fact that he had one ear missing peaked the curiosity of the youngsters at Iron River. Whenever he had his hair cut he requested the barber to leave a tuft of hair to cover the missing part. Rumor had it that he had been a Civil War soldier and had been clipped by a rebel bullet. Another tale held that he had lost it in a free-for-all lumberjack fight.

But Joel was neither a war veteran nor a descendent of a Revolutionary War family. The fact is that the Waters family were loyalists who fled to New Brunswick, Canada, when the Revolutionary War began. There they settled on a piece of land granted to loyal Britishers. In 1879 Joel migrated to Florence, Wisconsin, to seek better work and business opportunities in that new lumbering and mining country. There he operated a boarding and rooming house for lumberjacks and miners. A sober and upright man, he was outspoken about the immorality connected with the drinking and the sporting life of the rough community.

The rougher element of the little town were in turn outspoken about this "blue blood," whose family had fled the country in its battle for freedom from the redcoats and some of them resolved to "do him in."

WHEN PINE WAS KING

Late one night while Joel and his wife were sleeping upstairs and his three children, Byron, Harry and their little sister were sleeping downstairs, someone broke into their home. The intruder fumbled around in the dark until he reached the bed in which the children were sleeping and proceeded to crawl into the bed with them. Byron was sleeping on the outside of the bed and the ruffian pushed him onto the floor. The children screamed and Joel came down the stairs in his night shirt, carrying a lighted kerosene lamp above his head to see what the disturbance was all about. As Joel reached the bottom of the stairs the outlaw leaped upon him. The lamp crashed to the floor and set fire to the rag rug. As the men struggled desperately over the floor, Harry grabbed the lamp and rug and carried them out doors into the snow, then came back to help his father.

Joel was a little man and the burly lumberjack had him down with a strangle hold on his throat. Byron pummeled the intruder while Harry leaped on his back. As Joel was being worsted in the fight, Harry placed his fingers into the man's mouth and pulled out his cheeks with all his boyish strength. The lumberjack sank his teeth into Joel's ear and bit it through. The hold on the fellow's cheeks pulled him loose. He staggered up and ran out of the door. Joel went upstairs for his shotgun and ran out to find his assailant gone into the dark night. When the family assessed the damage they found Joel's ear hanging by a loose bit of skin. The doctor sewed it back on but it did not heal. Thereafter little Joel was the hero of the town but he always kept his ear covered by long hair.

CHAPTER TWENTY

Loaded with Dynamite

DYNAMITE was a useful thing to have in a lumber camp or on a river drive to blow out anchor banks for a new dam, blasting to clear a camp site or loosening a log jam in the river. For a boy of sixteen to carry a fifty pound box of blasting sticks over an Indian trail through the woods in the dark of night is a hazardous venture at best.

Dave Craig came from Canada to help his uncle Dan Coffin on his little farm cut out of the hardwoods near Iron River. Farm work occupied the young man only during the spring and summer. The lumber camps all around the area offered employment during the late fall and winter. Dave spent his first winter working for the Menominee River Lumber Company on the Brule River which is the dividing line between the UP and Wisconsin.

To the farm that spring came Old Louie Hunter, a shacker and recluse living in a small log cabin at the Reservoir Dam at the headwaters of the Brule.

"Old Louis," related Dave, "was a cantankerous critter. I never knew of his doing any work. I don't know how he lived—no doubt mostly on donations from lumber camp cooks and occasional fishermen and hunters who came his way. To carry a pail of water or an armload of wood was beneath his dignity.

"He was very excitable and nervous, perhaps due to the fact that he had a running cancer on his nose which he kept covered with court plaster. To see him stirring a batch of pancake dough and his nose dripping into it was enough to make one forget he was hungry for Louis' cakes. I used to watch him prance around and damn the grog shops but he wasn't very temperate himself. He could take a drink as well as the next fellow, especially if it were free.

"Well, he came to my uncle's farm one afternoon in the summer. I guess his supplies were low, judging from the way he wolfed the dinner my aunt set on the table for him. He was quite excited about a fifty pound box of dynamite that had been left when the log drive had passed that spring. It was there for the taking and Louis could sell it for a price if he got it near a buyer.

"He asked Uncle Dan to go with him to carry the box home.

" 'Louis,' said my uncle. 'You can see I've got a lot of hay down in the field and I've got to get it in before it rains. But this kid nephew of mine is a husky fellow. He can go with you to help carry it.'

"So I was the goat for Old Louis.

"The dam was thirty miles off in the woods. I had never used dynamite and I didn't feel too safe carrying fifty pounds of it on my back that distance.

"But off we started. We didn't even take a lunch along, figuring on getting something to eat along the road at one of the camps or at old man Pease's, a dam tender on the Brule. We reached Pease's shack at the end of twenty-five miles but found that Pease had left for town and had locked up his place. We slogged three miles more with Louis cussing all the way and came to the Menominee River Lumber Company camp.

"By this time Old Louis' tongue was hanging out for a drink and something to eat. The camp watchman was absent but there was a good store of food in the camp. Louis said he would make some biscuits and fry some bacon. He took a can off the shelf and mixed up a batter. He left it in the oven for an hour but it would not raise. As Louis was damning the stove the watchman came in to find his unexpected guests. Louis told him off for having such a poor bake oven.

" 'What did you use for baking powder? I don't have any in camp. I had to go to Iron River to get some.'

" 'Why, I got it out of that can on the shelf,' pointed Louis.

" 'I'll be shot for an old coot! That's arsenic, you damned fool. I keep it to poison wolves.'

"Well, we got a lunch to take us over the last few miles, never thinking it would be our last until we got back to Louis' shack. When we reached the little log cabin where the dynamite was stored we found that the cabin had been broken into and all the food stolen except a can of pancake flour and a few slices of rusty bacon. Too tired to eat I slept on a hard bunk without blankets while Louis paced the floor cursing the thieves.

"Next morning he started making pancakes—that was about all he ordinarily lived on. The place was blue with smoke leaking from the rickety old stove. As he was preparing breakfast he tore the dirty court plaster from his nose and replaced it with a new strip. After that sight, I couldn't eat any pancakes, which enraged the old man all the more.

" 'You're damned fussy. You'll see the day you'll be good and glad to eat my pancakes.'

"His prediction came true before that day was over.

"As we prepared to leave with the box of dynamite, we heard a low whining at the back of the shack. There we found a batch of two-week-old puppies which their mother had abandoned. Knowing that they would starve to death alone, we took them to the river and drowned them.

"Then we peeled some moosewood bark, the inner layer of which we used to make a tumpline with which to carry the heavy box. Placing the tumpline across my forehead, I set off with a glad goodbye on our thirty mile trip back through the woods and old logging trails, with the old man following empty-handed. The sun came out bright and the sweat rolled off my head and down my back under the fifty pound load. Louis jogged along but never once offered to spell me.

"No one was at the M.R.L. camp, so we went on. Our next stop was at the dugout of John the Bull, another recluse. In the middle of the road stood his two trained bulls, which he used to skid out logs and firewood. Hostile to strangers, the bulls bellowed and pawed the ground, their savage eyes rolling belligerently.

"I was in quite a predicament. With a box of dynamite on my back, I could neither run nor climb a tree. I had to do some tall walking and went around through the deep woods to get away, Louis running ahead of me, caring only for his own safety. My heart leaped into my throat and I could not call to him for help.

"We reached a lake where I eased off my pack and rested for thirty minutes. Resuming our journey we got to Pease's place, but it must have been the maid's day out, for the shack was still locked. So hungry, tired and a bit frightened, I adjusted the tumpline, left the supply road and struck off through the woods to Hagerman Lake. With one more rest within two miles of Louis' place I met up with a doe and two fawns. The doe started to run but the spotted little ones wouldn't follow her. I must have presented a curious sight to them. Off came my tumpline. I tried to catch one of the fawns. What I would have done with it, I didn't know, and what the mother would have done to me with her sharp hooves when it started to blat was another question.

"With this excitement to spur me on I shouldered my load again and reached Louis' home at 4:30 in the afternoon, tired out, hungry, my head and shoulders blistered, ten hours after starting out that morning, a feat I would not have undertaken in my prime. Youth is more ambitious than wise.

"Louis immediately started to stir up another pancake batter. Despite my fussiness and consciousness of the running nose, I wolfed down the cakes and complimented the old man on his cooking.

"John the Bull? Yes, he was a peculiar cuss too. Where he came from no one knew. He was called John the Trapper until he bought a pair of bull calves and trained them to work in a yoke. They were never castrated. When they reached maturity they weighed over a ton apiece. Ugly to strangers, they obeyed John's every command. He had but to whistle and they came to his cabin door. For forage they roamed the woods nearby and passersby gave them a wide berth.

"John came to the Brule River country as a young man, built a low log cabin, with a hole to crawl into it, no windows or doors. No one ever saw the inside of his place, for he kept strangers out and blocked the entrance with stones when he was inside. He never talked with strangers but would exchange a few words with old timers after knowing them for some time. It was believed that he had committed some crime in his youth and came there to evade the law. Whatever his secret was, it died with him.

"Passersby did not see him that summer. The bulls were seen tearing up the ground with their horns and bellowing for their master when a group of lumberjacks passed that way. The sheriff and his deputy investigated and found him dead in his retreat. Evidence pointed to the fact that he had died a natural death and that he had been dead several days.

"Driving the bulls away with clubs, the officers buried John the Bull on the river bank in his old dugout canoe. The bulls soon pawed the loose earth off the body and he had to be reburied under a mound of stone. One bull died of loneliness and the authorities sold the other to a Pentoga butcher—a ton of prime beef, no doubt.

"And so ended the peculiar career of the mystery man of the Brule River."

CHAPTER TWENTY-ONE

Honey for the Bear

WHILE THE majority of the men who settled in the UP worked in the woods or the mines, many found this type of rugged life too confining and too seasonal. A few chopped out little clearings to build a home and a little farm. Others lived off the land by hunting, fishing and trapping. Who is to say which were happiest and the more successful? Happiness was where men found it, be it in the rough camp, the hazardous mines or in a little shack in the woods where neighbors were few.

Joe LaBeouf preferred the lonely life of a shacker and wildlife hunter. His little log shanty held all he needed or wanted. Firewood was there for the cutting; the stream which flowing musically by his land gave him sweet speckled trout; deer and snowshoe rabbits supplied him meat and the sugar maple gave up its mellow syrup and succulent sugar. To fill out his larder of flour, bacon and salt, his traps supplied him with ready cash.

Bear trapping was Joe's long suit. He said to trap a bear, you had to think like a bear. Joe knew. He had trapped and shot 97 of them. But number 98 was his best accomplishment.

The boys were gathered around the hot stove discussing the weather prospects, whether the snow would be light enough to track a deer the next day, when the conversation turned to Joe LaBeouf and his success at bear trapping.

"Sure," commented Oscar Lundin, "Joe is a good bear man but there is one big fellow he will never get. That son-of-a-gun carried off one of my pigs last week, then came for another. I took a shot at him in the dark before he got in the pen but he got away."

So Joe was called in to try to get his number 98.

Joe was a man who could track a bear by his smell. He tried his conventional way of setting his huge toothed trap but number 98 sidestepped it but got away with the bait. His depredations mounted into hundreds of dollars of damage to stock, broken-in cabins and killing of does and fawns.

So Joe decided he had better begin to think like a bear. He set his trap at the bottom of a burned-out tree stump, high and hollow. He arranged a narrow slit down the inside, a sort of a doorway. Inside he suspended a pail of honey with holes punched in the bottom so the honey dripped down inside the stump, right onto the bear trap.

A logging chain led outside to a log six feet long and six inches through as a drag. The famous LaBeouf touch came at the doorway. Joe fastened a horizontal pole across the opening, just high enough so the bear would find it convenient to step over.

That night Joe sat under the drooping foliage of a hemlock tree two hundred feet from the set, rifle in hand and a flashlight in his pocket. He waited until the moon came up about eleven o'clock. The brush began to crackle in the woods. The noise came nearer and nearer. Joe gripped his rifle and waited. A huge black form emerged from the dark woods into the little clearing and approached the stump, its nostrils flaring to catch the sweet odor of honey.

Gingerly, cautiously, the bear stuck his head into the opening. Then quietly he raised his front foot and took a step inside. A vicious snap was followed by an unearthly howl and din that woke the echoes for miles around. With a bound the bear took off with the trap and the six foot log, cutting a swath through the surrounding brush, cracking off six inch poplar trees in his mad rush.

Cautiously Joe followed with his gun and flashlight in hand. The wild threshing stopped as the bear wound the chain about a small maple. Then all hell broke loose again. The bear was fast and told what he thought of his predicament. Joe crept closer and closer. Then raising his gun and sighting the flashlight along the barrel, he pressed the trigger. It was a clean shot. The brute went down in a cloud of flying dirt, to struggle a minute, then sink to the earth.

Too wise a trapper to try to skin a wounded bear in the dark, Joe sat on a stump and waited. Seeing no movement in the beam of his flashlight, and hearing no further sound, he took off to his cabin for the night.

It took two good horses to drag the great carcass to the cabin. Joe estimated that the black bear weighed over 400 pounds.

Number 98 was outsmarted by the man who thought like a bear.

Joe's next bear weighed less but gave him a chase which he long remembered. He had set a trap on an ant hill where bear had dug out their greatest delicacy, next to honey—ants and ant eggs. Joe hollowed out a small hole and placed his trap in it and covered it lightly with sand. To the trap he attached a small log which the bear could pull away, not heavy enough to allow him to pull out his paw.

The next morning Joe visited the trap and found it missing. There were unmistakable signs of a log being dragged through the brush and the tracks of great paws on the ground. Joe followed the signs until they brought him to the edge of a small lake and then disappeared. Wise to the ways of trapped bear, Joe looked around the shore of the lake and finally spotted a black object across the water. The lake was shallow, so he took off his trousers, shoes and underwear and with rifle in hand he waded into the water. The sun shone brightly and reflected on Joe's red beard and his red, hairy legs. Gradually he made his way until he saw his bear working madly at the trap and growling furiously. Taking careful aim, Joe planted a slug into the bear's neck. With a roar the beast rose on his hind legs and looked for his tormentor. Another well-placed shot brought him down where he lay in a foot of water.

For an easy, interesting and exciting life, Joe would not have traded places with timber kings and their wealth. His reputation as a bear hunter was worth more to him than gold.

CHAPTER TWENTY-TWO

The Preacher in the Lumber Camps

THERE WERE a few good spirits who were interested in the welfare and souls of the lumberjacks. While the average lumber camp operator was principally interested in using the jacks to get out as much timber for as low wages as possible and saloon keepers and bawdy houses ready and eager to fleece the men of their hard-earned money, a handful of others attempted to interest them in the better things of life.

Preacher Jim Roberts was one such. He was born in England and was preceded to Michigan by his father who worked in the iron mines at Ishpeming. At the age of twenty Jim was his father's partner underground for a year. He did not relish being "a bloody ground 'og" all his life, so he worked as a hoist man and surface man at the Lake Angeline mine for five years.

Being of a religious nature he served as local preacher for several years, working at the mines and preaching Sundays and evenings, until he was recommended by the Methodist District Superintendent to take a "charge." His first church was at Kenton. He studied the prescribed course laid out by the church and attended college during the summers until he became an ordained minister.

In the eyes of ministers at the yearly Michigan Methodist conferences an appointment to a church in the

UP was like a sentence to the salt mines. A far away land of crude villages and great stretches of wilderness, low salaries, indifferent congregations and flimsy parsonages, the UP held no attraction for ministers ambitious for large congregations, the refinements of civilization and educational opportunities for their children. Only recent graduates of theological seminaries, semi-lay preachers and those missionary-minded of the clergy were willing to accept a UP parish.

When at the yearly conferences of the church the UP was mentioned as a land of opportunity and challenge, ministers turned up their noses and accepted an assignment there only as a last resort.

When Bishop Fitzgerald observed the attitude of his ministers, he exclaimed to them:

"What is the matter with you men of God? To hear you talk and see you act one would think that the only way you can get to heaven is by the Southern Michigan route."

A man with his feet on the ground and his head in the clouds, Jim Roberts became interested in the spiritual welfare of the rough lumberjacks in the surrounding camps. He had beheld them come to town, wild for drink and recreation, to become the victims of men and women interested only in fleecing them of their hard earned cash. A lumberman named Dow of Marquette who owned camps in the vicinity of Kenton invited the preacher to speak at his camps. In the camps he ate with the men in the cook shacks. After the evening or Sunday meal the dining tables were cleared back and the benches arranged around the cook shack walls. Dow invited the men to come in and introduced the speaker. Most of them

READY FOR THE SPRING DRIVE

Only the hardiest, most skillful, the most reckless men were hired to withstand the rigors of "river-hog" work.

Burton Historical Collection.

WAIST-DEEP IN ICY WATERS
"River hogs" break up a log jam with pike poles, peavies and dynamite.
Burton Historical Collection.

THE WANIGAN

The cook shack was built on rafts and kept up with the crew as they worked the logs down the river to the mill.

Burton Historical Collection.

LUMBER CAMP PREACHERS
Rev. James Roberts, Lumberjack Preacher. His parish was the lumber camps, the small mill towns and the scattered farms in the U.P.

MAY THE TRUEST JOYS OF CHRISTMAS BE YOURS, SINCERELY, ARCHDEACON AND MRS. POYSEOR.

ARCHDEACON W. POYSEOR TRAVELED NEARLY 400 MILES WITH THESE DOGS DURING THE WINTER OF 1896.

"Holy Bill," as he was called by the lumberjacks, Rev. Poyseor's parish was the lumber camps in the U.P.
Courtesy Mrs. Thomas Mudge

attended the services, giving respectful attention. At one camp a free-thinker scoffed openly at his preaching. After the service some of the men asked Roberts if they should run the disturber out of camp, but he asked for Christian tolerance. The man later became a regular attendant at the preaching.

At times 100 or more men ranged around the walls of the cook shack, sang songs led by the minister on his concertina or fiddle, singing some of the old gospel favorites like "What a Friend I Have in Jesus," "The Old Rugged Cross," and "Throw Out the Lifeline," which the men had not heard since boyhood. Roberts discovered that some of the jacks had had a good family and church background but under the influence of the camps had drifted away from their early home training.

After the services Dow went from one man to another with a slip of paper and asked them how much they wanted to donate to the preacher. They usually gave from five cents to a quarter. These donations Dow deducted from their pay at the end of the season, added a liberal amount himself and gave Roberts a check which sometimes amounted from $15.00 to $20.00, a large sum, considering that his own salary was only a few hundred dollars a year. Dow believed that this preaching was a strong morale builder and resulted in the men drinking less liquor and saving their pay as well as producing more logs at the river landing.

The Reverend conducted communion services at times and witnessed men with tears in their eyes take the "cup and the bread" for the first time since they left their home church as boys.

The mill town of Sidnaw was located 12 miles from

Kenton, connected by a crooked wagon road and seven miles of rail. A lumberjack died at Sidnaw and Roberts was asked to conduct the funeral service. The temperature had dropped to 15 below zero and a great blizzard was in progress, blocking the wagon road. A telegram arrived requesting him to start walking on the railroad track and stating that a pump handcar with a crew of four men would attempt to buck the two foot snowdrifts and meet him part way. He started out on foot into the face of the driving storm and dropping temperature. On and on he trudged, lifting his felt-and-rubber shod feet over the snow, looking through the blinding gale for a sight of the handcar and the men coming to his rescue. As he walked he saw tracks of a pack of timber wolves crossing ahead of him. With visions of falling exhausted in the deep snow and being devoured by the ravenous wolves, he finally staggered to the little church two hours late for the service. The handcar had stuck in a ravine behind a six foot drift and the men had abandoned the car and walked back to Sidnaw. The funeral party had waited. The corpse was properly laid at rest in the frozen ground in the little cemetery which was the final resting place for countless homeless lumberjacks.

Preacher Roberts stayed on for several years to baptize, marry and bury many other men, women and children in that isolated, rugged community. One was old Joe White, a colored Civil War veteran, who ran a barbershop in Kenton. Joe had on occasion made small contributions to the little Methodist Church and was particularly liberal when under the influence of strong liquor. Roberts was active in bringing about prohibition in the county and made the rounds of the town to collect contributions for the cause. Joe saw the preacher going from store to store and from residence to residence with his subscription book in hand. The old pensioner, who was receiving his dollar a day from the government, asked what the preacher was up to. When he was informed that he was trying to dry up the county, Joe shouted that he would never give the church another cent.

Not long after this incident the colored barber was found lying on the floor of his little shop with a heart attack. He was not discovered for three days when some of his cronies saw him and lifted him onto a couch in the back of the shop. To revive him they poured whiskey down his throat. When their efforts failed to bring the old man to consciousness they left him there to die. His body lay on the couch for three more days without anyone touching him. When township supervisor Shingler learned about it, he called in Roberts. They found Joe in a very ripe condition in his besmeared clothing. Together they cut off his clothing and underwear. His body was bloated beyond recognition. Shingler bought a suit of underwear and a suit of clothes and shirt and they covered him as best they could under the conditions. The Supervisor sent down a rough box made of pine boards at the mill. Neighbors helped place the body in the box and hauled it on a horse-drawn wagon to the cemetery a mile and a half for burial. The ground was frozen hard. The men dug a grave. When they reached gravel, the earth kept caving in as fast as they dug. They excavated a nine foot hole and stood the rough box on end and threw back the gravel to cover it. Joe went into his everlasting resting place standing up.

The little English preacher whom Joe refused to help

in his prohibition cause preached the funeral service over the remains. White had enough money left from his pension check to pay for the funeral expenses with $20.00 over, which Shingler gave to the minister.

A few of the lumberjacks were married and their heavy drinking was a burden of shame for their families. Bill Handy was one. His system had become so sodden with liquor that he lost all interest in his family and spent his time mooching drinks from saloon to saloon. His little wife found it necessary to work as a hired girl to feed and clothe the children. Her work at home, her working out and her worry over the family and her husband's drinking brought about her physical collapse and early death.

At the funeral services which Roberts conducted in the little Methodist Church, Bill Hart, the station agent and one of the pallbearers, pointed to Handy and remarked:

"You killed her! You neglected her!"

Handy took the accusation deeply to heart. He began to go over his past conduct with a guilty conscience. His wife had been a spiritualist and he feared a visitation from her. Rev. Roberts met him on the street and asked him where he had been. His eyes bloodshot and his face bloated, Handy replied:—

"I've been out to the graveyard kneeling on my wife's grave. I asked her if I was to blame for her dying. I got no satisfaction—got no answer. I'm going to kill that Hart for what he said at the funeral."

Roberts warned Hart who set up every precaution to avoid Handy thereafter. Soon, Hart, at his own request, was moved to another depot in a neighboring town. No harm came to him but Handy kept up his hard drinking until he died a few years later of alcoholism and remorse. His children were left "on the town."

Rev. Roberts started his ministry with two charges, at Kenton and at Sidnaw. He gradually developed preaching services in three other communities in the lumber region, at Ewen, Bruce's Crossing and Bergland. He frequently preached at Maple Grove in the town hall and at Merriweather in the school house.

The minister's salary came from missionary money of the Methodist Churches of Michigan. As the area developed and his preaching attracted more support the income increased until his churches became self-supporting and finally was sufficient to pay back the money advanced from the state church funds.

However, few people gave much to the church. One lumber operator gave $2.00 a week but most of the members were poor. There was no tithing and no large gifts. The minister's salary was supplemented by donations of vegetables from farms and gardens of parishioners. Chickens, pieces of beef and pork after the fall butchering and an occasional venison roast were brought to the parsonage by people who had no cash to spare.

Lumberman Jensen had acquired a cow and told Roberts he could have half of the milk for the milking. Harvest festivals were held at the churches to raise money for the treasuries. Farmers brought vegetables, meat and loads of wood, women made quilts and knitwear, merchants donated canned food to be sold at the festivals for the church. At one festival Rev. Roberts was given a pig, which escaped and had the whole community chasing it.

The little church at Ewen lay in a swamp. When it

rained planks had to be laid down to enable the attendants to enter. A big box stove with a long stovepipe running under the ceiling heated the edifice. The church was later moved to higher ground and used many years thereafter.

To come closer to his parishioners, Roberts often went out to outlying farms to help with the haying when labor was scarce. He cut hardwood on shares to heat the church and parsonage, hauled the wood in on horsedrawn sleighs and stacked it in the church yard and woodshed behind his dwelling. During the depression Roberts found himself the minister of the Methodist Church in Munising. Money for his salary was scarce. He persuaded the Cleveland-Cliffs Iron Mining Company to give him permission to cut wood for the church on their property. The Company placed a flatcar at the scene of the cutting. Roberts roused local church members from their beds each morning to take them to the woods to cut logs into four foot sections and load them on the flatcar. Women members prepared and sent along lunches for the crew.

The minister had a difficult time getting enough volunteers but finally they brought sixty cords to town and had it hauled to the church yard with teams and sleighs and buzzed it into stove lengths. The total cash cost for the job was only $4.00 for gasoline.

One day as Roberts was out looking for volunteers to help with the buzzing, he met one of the town characters in a Model T with his dog and gun.

"We're having a buzzing bee at the church and the ladies are getting up a big dinner. Will you come over and help?"

The character was thinking as fast as the preacher

was talking and finally shifting his quid of tobacco from one cheek to the other, replied in a lazy drawl:

"Wall, I'd help you but I was goin' huntin' and I don't want to dissypoint my dog."

Archdeacon William Poyseor was a circuit rider via pony and dog team for the Episcopal Church in the small lumber towns in the UP with his home and headquarters at Crystal Falls. Called "Holy Bill" by the lumber men, he preached in the camps and all of the churches in his circuit. He started as a missionary preacher in 1895 and served his scattered flock wherever he found them, in towns, farms and the woods. In the spring, summer and fall he traversed the trails and rutted roads from place to place on the back of an Indian pony. He lived with his parishioners as he went. For a man who ate so many chickens and good food in their homes, he was still a spare, slim man, hard muscled from his long trips, affable and well-loved. He had come over from Wales and his missionary zeal burned bright. No call for help or spiritual comfort was too far away. He stayed at death beds, buried its victims, baptized children and married couples. Never one to count the cost or weigh the salary, he served wherever he was needed, in homes, lumber camps and in churches along the way. When winter blizzards blocked travel for his pony, he hitched two dogs to his sleigh and took off. One winter he traveled over 400 miles by dog team to visit the outlying families, the camps and the scattered churches in his wide parish. For his many years of work and devotion Bishop Mott Williams of the Episcopal Diocese ordained Rev. Poyseor "Archdeacon." So great was the Bishop's love and admiration for the thin little man that he set aside enough money in his will to

WHEN PINE WAS KING

enable the Archdeacon to return to his native Wales to visit relatives and friends.

So the men, women and children of that rough country during the cutting and ravaging of the pine land were not entirely left to the mercy of the human wolves who sought to ravage their bodies, purses and hearts. A surprising number of the youth of those small, now-desolated villages caught a spark from these lumber camp preachers, moved on to gain education and fame and reputation in broader fields. There were other men of God, in addition to Reverend Jim and "Holy Bill," who had left ease, position and the comforts of civilization to serve in an area where spiritual rewards were more substantial than were creature comforts.

Supplement

Lumberjack Terms

PARBUCKLE—A decking chain to roll logs onto a pile.

CROSS HAUL—A road used by a team of horses in decking logs.

DECK—A pile of logs on a skidway.

SKIDWAY—Where the logs were rolled or piled up before hauling.

ROUND TURN—Where the big log sleighs were turned around.

COAL OIL—Kerosene.

SKY PILOT—A traveling preacher who visited the camps.

JAM BOOK—There is no such thing.

KEG LOG—A log which was jammed in the river bed and caused a pileup.

THROW A SNAG INTO A LOG—Push or hold one end of a log to keep it even.

SKID—Logs or trees laid parallel on which logs were decked or piled.

CANADA A LOG—Prying one end of a log ahead with a cant hook to push it forward or back.

ROSS A LOG—Peeling bark off one side of a log to make it slip along more easily in skidding.

SHORT STUFF—Short pieces of logs.

HOT LOGGING—Cutting, skidding and hauling at the same time.

WHEN PINE WAS KING

VAN—The camp store which sold tobacco, clothing and lumberjack supplies.

WANIGAN—A cook camp built on a raft used on a river drive.

WINDFALL—Timber blown down.

NOSE BAG—A sack in which a jack carried his lunch, or a feed bag which was tied over horses' nose.

WING—A bunch of logs hung up by an obstruction in the river.

CENTER—Logs piled up in the middle of a river on a rock or sunken log.

DEADHEAD—A log which would not float.

POLING—Keeping logs going straight in the current at dams by means of a pike pole.

PIKE POLE—A pole from 12 to 16 feet long with a spike at the end and a side hook used to push or pull logs in the river.

SACKING—Getting the logs back into the river after they have been left high and dry in the floods.

RIVER HOGS or RIVER PIGS—Men driving logs down the river.

CEDAR SAVAGES—Men cutting short stuff.

BUNK—Either a bed in the bunkhouse or the two cross beams on which logs are piled on a sleigh.

SNAKING—Skidding or dragging a log over the ground.

FOUND—Meals in camp.

BREAKUP—The end of cutting when warm spring weather made it impossible to operate.

PIECE WORK—Cutting fence poles or railroad ties or cedar poles by the piece rather than by the day.

CHICADEE—A road monkey whose duty it was to shovel horse manure off the hauling roads.

LUMBERJACK TERMS

CRUMB CHASER—A lumberjack picking lice and bedbugs out of his clothes.

TRAVELING DANDRUFF—Lice.

GRAPEFRUIT—Cold canned tomatoes.

MORNING GLORIES—Flapjacks or pancakes served every breakfast.

COLDSHUT—A single link of chain used to repair a broken chain, soft enough to be closed with a hammer without heat.

SOWBELLY—Fat pork pickled in brine and served daily.

REDHORSE—Pickled beef.

SOFTASS—A sack of hay used as a teamster's seat.

BULLPEN—A crowded sleeping cabin or bunkhouse.

BILL STUFF—A cedar log 10 feet to 20 feet long.

DEACON SEAT—A wooden bench at the end of a bunkhouse occupied by the oldtimers and the best story tellers in camp.

MUZZLE LOADERS—Sleeping bunks into which lumberjacks entered from the end, sometimes three tiers high.

BITCHES or JOBBER'S SUNS—Kerosene torches used for night work.

BRIER—A saw.

JETHRO—A long steel-shod pole used in prying logs to loosen them off a sleigh or car.

CORNER BINDS—Chains used to fasten the outside logs on a bunk at each end of a sleigh.

WRAPPER—A chain used to bind around the entire load of logs.

BEAR TRAP—A set of chains used to tighten the wrapper.

PIG IRON—Any kind of log which would not float.

SWAMP HOOK—A hook used at the end of a decking chain or line to secure it in a log.

TOTE TEAM—A team of horses used to haul supplies to the camp.

TOTE ROAD—A road used to haul supplies over.

HAY BURNERS—A term used by the disrespectful when referring to horses.

MULE SKINNER—Any teamster.

BULLWACKER—An oxen driver.

WORK TRAIL—A road used to drive a team from the camp to the cuttings.

CORDUROY—Poles or logs laid across a swampy spot in the road or over a small stream.

POLE TRAIL—A trail over which the river hogs could walk along a river during the spring drive. Poles or logs were dropped over streams or backwater for the men to walk over.

GO-DEVIL—A travois used in skidding logs out of the woods.

SKIDDING TONGS—Steel tongs, like ice tongs, which clamped the end of a log to skid it out of the woods.

CHUCK—Food at the camp.

GREENHORN—A city dude or inexperienced person working in the camp for the first time or a recent immigrant.

NOTE: These terms were furnished by the author and C. J. Sawyer of the Sawyer-Stoll Timber Company of Escanaba.

Some Logging Companies Which Operated in the UP

Isaac Stephenson Lumber Company
Ford River Lumber Company
Stack Lumber Company
Spaulding Lumber Company
Stickney-Johnson Lumber Company
Dan McLeod Lumber Company
Hall and Munson Lumber Company
Spaulding, Houghteling and Johnson Lumber Company
Wisconsin Land and Lumber Company
Bob Dollar Lumber Company
Cleveland-Cliffs Iron Mining Company
Hitchcock and Bailey Lumber Company
J. M. Longyear Company
Menominee River Lumber Company
Northwestern Cooperage and Lumber Company
Bay de Noc Lumber Company
Bonifas Lumber Company
United Lumber Company
Sawyer-Stoll Lumber Company
Peacock and Farrell Lumber Company
Madden and Schaible Lumber Company
Ramsey and Jones Lumber Company
Cook Brothers Lumber Company

P. C. Fuller Lumber Company
Sawyer-Goodman Lumber Company
Herman Holmes Lumber Company
Von Platen-Fox Lumber Company
G. W. Wells Lumber Company
Alger-Smith Lumber Company
Conn-Mitchell Lumber Company
Quinnesec Logging Company
Menominee River Boom Company
Knapp-Stout and Company
Chicago Lumber Company
Fryant, Fuller and White Lumber Company

Lumberjack Songs

As Sung By

JIM MURPHY
TIMBER CRUISER
AND CAMP FOREMAN

My Willie Oh!

Come all you lovers, young and handsome, loud in vain
 to you I'll sing,
For the losing of my Willie,—he has gone to serve his
 king;
He has gone on board of the tender to somewhere I don't
 know,
But may the angels still protect him. Send to me my
 Willie, oh!

Had I the gold that's in the Indies, rich Peru or Mexico,
Unto the king I'd resign it for my Willie, don't you know.
For seven long years I've been daily writing to the Bay
 of Biscay
Until pale death brought me answer from my Willie, don't
 you know.

As I lay sleeping he came weeping to my chamber door
 so low,
Saying "Mary dear, don't be frightened, for I'm the ghost
 of your Willie, oh.
Where are those rosy cheeks so lovely not very long ago.
Oh, it was the sea that stained my color for I'm the ghost
 of your Willie, oh.

"Three stormy days and stormy nights we tossed upon
 the raging main;
It's long we strove our bark to save, but all our striving
 was in vain.

Even then when ere I chilled my blood my heart was filled
   with love to thee,
But the storm is o'er and I' at rest, so Mary weep no more
   for me."

That whole long night we sat discoursing about our love
   some time ago,
Saying "Mary, dear, I must be going, for the cocks shall
   shortly crow."
When Mary saw him disappearing down her cheeks the
   tears did flow,
Saying "Now I'll leave this handsome city to some lonesome grave I'll go,
And there I'll spend my days in mourning, for my Willie
   don't you know."

The State of Arkansaw

Oh, in 1869 in the merry month of June,
I landed in vanzousi one sultry afternoon.
Up stepped a walking skeleton with his long and lantern
   jaw
And invited me to his hotel in the state of Arkansaw.
I followed up this great big bloke until his dwelling place,
Sure poverty was depicted on his dirty, baggy face.
He fed me on corn diggers and meat I couldn't chaw,
And fifty cents he taxed for this in the state of Arkansaw.

I was to rise next morning to catch an early train.
He says "you had better stay with me my lad.
I've got some land to drain.
I'll give you fifty cents a day, your washing, board and all,
And you'll find you'll be a different lad when you leave
   Arkansaw."

I hired out there to this big bloke,
Van Justice was his name.
He was six feet, seven in his sock,
And thin as any crane.
His hair hang down in rat tails around his lantern jaw.
He was a photograph of all the gents in the state of Arkansaw.

Oh, in 1871 I dread the memory still.
I shook the boots right off my feet with a cursed and blasted chill.
I got so thin upon sage and sassafras
I could hide behind a straw
And you bet I was a different lad
When I left Arkansaw.

So here's a health to your swamp angels,
Your cane brakes and your chills;
Likewise your sage and sassafras
And your corn dodger pills.
If ever I do go that way I'll give to you my paw,
But it will be through a telescope
That I'll see Arkansaw.

I started out next morning
To walk to Little Rock.
My teeth began to loosen
And my knees began to knock.
I staggered into a saloon
And called for whiskey raw
And I got drunk as a son of a gun
When I left Arkansaw.

The Stowaway

From Liverpool across the Atlantic our good ship was sailing deep,
With the sky bright with sunshine and the waters beneath us asleep.
Not a bad tempered man was among us. A jollier crew never sailed,
Except the first mate—a bit of a savage but good seaman as ever sailed.

Regulation and order his motto—strong as iron, both steady and quick,
With a pair of big bushy black eyebrows and eyes fierce as those of old nick.
He came from below one bright morning grasping a lad by the arm,
A poor little golden haired urchin who had ought to be home with his mam.

And the mate asked the lad rather roughly how he came to be stowing away,
Cheating the owners and captain, eating, sailing and all without pay.
Then the lad with a face bright and winning and charming blue eyes like a girl's,
Looked up at the scowling first mate, lads, and shook back his long golden curls.

And he says in a voice clear and pretty: "My stepmother put me aboard
And she hid me away down the stairs there, to keep me she couldn't afford.

And she said that the good ship would take me to Halifax
town, oh, so far,
And she says the good Lord is your father. He lives
where the good angels are.

"It's a lie," says the mate. "Not your mother but some
of those big skulkers here,
Some soft hearted milk bearded sailor. Speak up, tell the
truth, do you hear?"
Then spoke up another old sailor to the mate who seemed
staggered himself:
"Let him go over to old Nova Scotia and I'll work out his
passage myself."

"Belay," says the mate. "Shut your mouth, man, I'll sail
this here craft, bet your life,
And I'll fit the lie out of him somehow, just as square as
a fork fits a knife."
And he plants him before amidships, his eyes like two coals
Then knitting his black brows in anger he tumbled the
poor lad below,
Saying "perhaps by tomorrow twill change you. If not
back to England you'll go."

I'm as rough and as hardened old sailor as any blue jacket
afloat,
But the salt water sprang to my eyes, lad, and I left the
best wish in my throat.
I took him some dinner, be sure lads, just to think, only
nine years of age.
And the next morning the six bells were tolling when the
mate fetched him out of his cage.

WHEN PINE WAS KING

And he plants him before amidships, his eyes like two coals alight,
And his teeth they were set mad with passion and his hand lifted, ready to smite.
"Tell the truth, lad, and then I'll forgive you, but the truth I must have, speak out.
It was not your mother that brought you, but some of these men here about.

Then the lad with a face bright and winning, clear and shining with innocent youth.
He looked up at the scowling first mate, lads, and says: "Sir, I've told you the truth."
It was clear the mate wouldn't believe him, though everyone else did on board.
With rough hand by the shoulder he seized him and says: "You shall hang, by Lord."

Then he pulled out his watch from his pocket just as if he'd been drawing a knife.
"If in ten minutes more you don't speak, lad, there's a rope and good bye to your life."
He stood like a figure of marble his watch tightly clasped in his hand
And the passengers all still around him, ne'er the like on the sea or the land.

Oh, you never did see such a sight, lads, as the lad with the bright, pretty face,
Proud though steady with courage never of asking for grace.

Eight minutes went by all in silence. Says the mate:
"Speak up, lad, have your say."
And the tear drops they fell from his eyes, lads, and he falteringly asked: "May I pray?"

The mate kind of trembled and shivered and nodded his head in reply,
Though his face was all white of a sudden; the hot light was in his eye.
The little lad knelt on the deck, then, his hands clasped over his breast
As he must have done often at home, lads, at night time when going to rest.

Then it's soft came the first words: "Our Father," soft and low from those baby lips.
Though low, they were heard like a trumpet by each tar on board of that ship.
Every bit of that prayer he goes through with to "Ever and Ever, Amen,"
And for all the bright gold in the Indies, I wouldn't have heard it again.

Then he said as he finished up rising and casting his blue eyes above:
"Kind Father, oh take me to heaven, back again to my own mother's love."
For a minute or two like true magic we stood every man like the dead.
When back to the mate's face came rushing the lifeblood again warm and red.
Like a man says the mate: "God forgive me that ever I used you so bad."

Off his feet was that lad sudden lifted and clasped to the mate's rugged breast
And a husky voice whispered: "God bless you," as his lips to his forehead he pressed.
"You believe me, then, sir?" asked the youngster. "Believe you," he kissed him once more.
"You have laid down your life for the truth, lad, I'd believe you from now evermore!"
In his arms to the cabin he bore him and all through the rest of the trip,
We worshiped him just like an idol, the pride and the pet of the ship.

Tall Tales of Taylor

By Lloyd Frank Merrell
Lumber Camp Preacher

A hollow pine on Taquamenon
Was used to bridge the stream.
Del was haulin's a load o' logs to
    the mill
An' met a team.

Of course this mighty timber
Had every log outclassed—
The space inside—stupendous—
And all the knot-hole, vast—
Del backed his load into one
An' let the team go past.

When Del was rafting timber,
He yelled one night at the mate,
"Can't you see that log bobbing up
An' down out in the wake?"

"Ride 'er to port, river-hog—
It's loose from its moorin' pin."
Del found at the dock he'd ridden
The shadow o' the smoke-stack in.